Cambridge Elements ≡

Elements in Eighteenth-Century Connections
edited by
Eve Tavor Bannet
University of Oklahoma
Markman Ellis
Queen Mary University of London

THE DOMINO AND THE EIGHTEENTH-CENTURY LONDON MASQUERADE

A Social Biography of a Costume

Meghan Kobza
Newcastle University

CAMBRIDGE
UNIVERSITY PRESS

Shaftesbury Road, Cambridge CB2 8EA, United Kingdom

One Liberty Plaza, 20th Floor, New York, NY 10006, USA

477 Williamstown Road, Port Melbourne, VIC 3207, Australia

314–321, 3rd Floor, Plot 3, Splendor Forum, Jasola District Centre,
New Delhi – 110025, India

103 Penang Road, #05–06/07, Visioncrest Commercial, Singapore 238467

Cambridge University Press is part of Cambridge University Press & Assessment,
a department of the University of Cambridge.

We share the University's mission to contribute to society through the pursuit of
education, learning and research at the highest international levels of excellence.

www.cambridge.org
Information on this title: www.cambridge.org/9781009468244

DOI: 10.1017/9781009042406

First published 2023

A catalogue record for this publication is available from the British Library

ISBN 978-1-009-46824-4 Hardback
ISBN 978-1-009-04555-1 Paperback
ISSN 2632-5578 (online)
ISSN 2632-556X (print)

The Domino and the Eighteenth-Century London Masquerade

A Social Biography of a Costume

Elements in Eighteenth-Century Connections

DOI: 10.1017/9781009042406
First published online: November 2023

Meghan Kobza
Newcastle University

Author for correspondence: Meghan Kobza, meg.kobza@ncl.ac.uk

Abstract: This Element presents new cultural, social, and economic perspectives on the eighteenth-century London masquerade through an in-depth analysis of the classic domino costume. Constructing the object biography of the domino through material, visual, and written sources brings together various experiences of the masquerade and expands the existing geographical, chronological, and socio-economic scope of the entertainment beyond the masquerade event itself. This Element examines the domino's physical and figurative movements from the masquerade warehouse, through eighteenth-century fashionable society, and into print and visual culture. It draws upon masquerade warehouse records, newspapers, manuscripts, prints, and physical objects to establish a comprehensive understanding of the domino and how it reflected contemporary experiences of the real and imagined masquerade. Analysing the domino through interdisciplinary methodologies illustrates the impact material and visual sources can have on reshaping existing scholarship.

Keywords: masquerade, costume, warehouse industry, material culture, consumer history

ISBNs: 9781009468244 (HB), 9781009045551 (PB), 9781009042406 (OC)
ISSNs: 2632-5578 (online), 2632-556X (print)

Contents

Introduction

Eighteenth-century Britain witnessed the development of a very specific and popular form of social entertainment – the masquerade. These costumed entertainments operated as either private events (to invited guests) or large commercial entertainments (available for the price of a ticket). A combination of regular reports in newspapers and descriptive fictional masquerades in popular literature spread textual depictions of the entertainment throughout the Georgian world, bringing ostentatious costumes and themes of revelry and debauchery to the reading public. The excitement of this glittering entertainment was further amplified in contemporary visual and material culture with illustrations of lively masquerade scenes filled with creative, humorous, and fancy disguises filling print shop windows, appearing on handkerchiefs, and taking shape in decorative and cosmetic porcelain figurines. These representations helped recreate the evening's entertainment and engaged the wider public with the culture of the masquerade, often mixing fantasy with reality and leaving the imagination to fill the spaces between. Within these gaps between textual and visual and material depictions, there is a noticeable discrepancy concerning an integral symbol and component of the masquerade: the domino. The domino habit – consisting of a cloak, mask, and usually tricorn hat with feathers – was both everywhere and nowhere. It was repeatedly presented as problematic across newspaper sources, used as a profitable tool among masquerade warehouse owners, and the convenient costume of choice for gentlemen of the upper ranks, all while remaining noticeably absent from visual depictions.

Exploring the complex life of the domino and its dichotomous nature through a variety of material, visual, and written sources, including existing domino habits, warehouse inventories, trade cards, diaries and correspondence, prints, and newspapers allows us to re-examine the domino's place within Georgian culture and how its relationship to the masquerade sheds new light on the lived experience and historical significance of the masquerade as a cultural phenomenon. Using this combination of sources establishes a more comprehensive understanding of the domino and how it reflected real and imagined experiences of the masquerade. The Element will first establish a definition of the domino and examine its materiality and physicality before moving on to two subsequent sections. These sections will trace the domino's movements through eighteenth-century society – from the warehouse to the masquerade to print and visual cultures. Following the domino through these various spaces and contexts will answer key research questions regarding how the domino was worn, how it contributed to the socio-economic exclusivity of the masquerade, why it was a popular costume choice, and how its meaning and purpose changed as it moved into different spaces. It will examine contrasting representations of the domino found in masquerade reports and imagery that circulated through the public sphere. Newspapers presented the domino as an overwhelming and dull presence across masquerades while the domino remained largely absent from contemporary visual culture. The range in sources also provides important insight into what the domino meant to people of various situations: seller versus consumer, middling versus upper rank, hosts versus participant. Ultimately, this Element will expand the chronological, geographical, and socio-economic footprint of the masquerade, bringing in the perspectives of understudied contributors to the masquerade experience (warehousemen and women, masquerade hosts) and examining the entertainment as the domino existed across time (the days leading up to and following the masquerade itself) and moved through London (from vendor to wearer to masquerade and back again). Employing material and visual cultures to analyse the domino will revise and broaden existing historical narratives and literary scholarship on the masquerade, widening our understanding of the contemporary cultural and social significance of the entertainment.

Existing scholarship on the masquerade, including the work of Terry Castle, Catherine Craft-Fairchild, and Dror Wahrman, examines the entertainment in and of itself and the opportunities it provided for various types of social interactions.[1] Their work engages heavily with literary sources, leaving important material in manuscript accounts, material culture, and visual culture understudied. Dress historian Aileen Ribeiro has produced significant research on the masquerade habit in England and its appearance and function in portraiture. Her work on eighteenth-century dress has supplied a concise history of the domino costume, explaining its Italian roots and contemporary presence in masquerade culture.[2] Her work, however, leaves room for further analysis of the domino as it existed in wider cultural, social, and economic contexts. Examining the nuances of the masquerade through text and the material and visual culture of the domino will provide a more comprehensive understanding of the cultural, social, and economic aspects of the masquerade. The domino highlights the tension between real experiences of the masquerade and imagined expectations

---

[1] Terry Castle, *Masquerade and Civilization: The Carnivalesque in Eighteenth-Century English Culture and Fiction* (Stanford: Stanford University Press, 1986); Catherine Craft-Fairchild, *Masquerade and Gender: Disguise and Female Identity in Eighteenth-Century Fictions by Women* (Pennsylvania: Pennsylvania State University Press, 1993); John Eglin, *Venice Transfigured: The Myth of Venice in British Culture, 1660–1797* (New York: Palgrave, 2001); Dror Wahrman, *The Making of the Modern Self: Identity and Culture in Eighteenth-Century England* (London: Yale University Press, 2006).

[2] Aileen Ribeiro, *The Dress Worn at Masquerades in England, 1730 to 1790, and Its Relation to Fancy Dress in Portraiture* (London: Garland Publishing, 1984), 33–9; Aileen Ribeiro, *Dress in Eighteenth-Century Europe: 1715–1789* (London: Yale University Press, 2002), 245–50.

of the entertainment as depicted in visual culture and literature. As Amanda Vickery, Giorgio Ricllo, and many other scholars of eighteenth-century material culture have argued, objects can and should be used as evidence in combination with written and visual sources. Subsequent work in eighteenth-century material culture by Vickery, Zara Anishanslin, and Jennifer Van Horn, among others, has skilfully combined material culture and historiographical methodologies to create object biographies, presenting more complete pictures of objects' significance in social and cultural contexts.[3] Riello's 'history of things' approach serves as the primary methodology used, as it is most suited to this Element and the surviving evidence and sources, providing a historical analysis of the relationship between the domino and people, as well as exploring how the domino and the masquerade operated in Georgian society in both real and figurative ways.

1 The Masquerade and the Domino

1.1 The London Masquerade

The eighteenth-century London masquerade has been characterised as a space for social mixing and debauchery, open to all individuals, irrespective of social rank. While their use in contemporary literature and visual culture supports this perspective, recent work on the social history of the entertainment has shown that it was much more complex than these representations suggest. Analyses of the financial aspects of attending a masquerade, the spaces in which they were held, and ticketing practices all reveal that this entertainment did not align with wider trends of increasing accessibility that other forms of leisure culture experienced.[4] Rather, the masquerade remained an exclusive space of elite sociability that reinforced the shifting social hierarchies of the eighteenth century through fashionable display and conspicuous consumption. The availability

---

[3] Giorgio Riello, 'Things that Shape History: Material Culture and Historical Narratives', in *History and Material Culture: A Student's Guide to Approaching Alternative Sources*, ed. Karen Harvey (Routledge, 2009), 24–47, 28; John Styles and Amanda Vickery, eds., *Gender, Taste, and Material Culture in Britain and North America 1700–1830* (New Haven: Yale University Press, 2006); Zara Anishanslin, *Portrait of a Woman in Silk: Hidden Histories of the British Atlantic World* (New Haven: Yale University Press, 2016); Jennifer Van Horn, *The Power of Objects in Eighteenth-Century British America* (Chapel Hill: University of North Carolina Press, 2017).

[4] Peter Borsay, 'The Emergence of a Leisure Town: Or an Urban Renaissance?', *Past & Present* 126 (February 1990): 189–96, www.jstor.org/stable/650813; Neil McKendrick, 'The Consumer Revolution of Eighteenth-Century England', in *The Birth of a Consumer Society: The Commercialization of Eighteenth-Century England*, ed. John Brewer, Neil McKendrick, and J. H. Plumb (London: Europa, 1982), 9–21; John Brewer, *The Pleasures of the Imagination: English Culture in the Eighteenth Century* (London: HarperCollins, 1997); Meghan Kobza, 'Dazzling or Fantastically Dull? Re-examining the Eighteenth-Century London Masquerade', *Journal for Eighteenth-Century Studies* 43, no. 2 (2020): 161–81.

of tickets did not promise affordability or mingling between ranks nor did costumes guarantee gender play or transgression of social boundaries in dress. The chronological framework of the masquerade is equally important in considering its place within leisure culture. This Element examines the domino within the second half of the eighteenth century, 1762 to 1810, placing it in the context of two distinct periods: the height of masquerade culture and its gradual move to wider accessibility through the adoption of broader commercial practices. The first period fell within the height of masquerade fashionableness between 1762 and 1785 and was defined by extortionate ticket prices, ostentatious costumes, and spectacle. Tickets cost an average of two guineas (excluding the cost of costume and transportation), making them reasonably affordable for only 0.8 per cent of the population and the highest priced in leisure culture.[5] The masquerade's horizontal movement between elite spaces of sociability and the presence of guards at the doors at this time reinforced the exclusionary nature of the entertainment, allowing the nobility and gentry, as well as key members of the *beau monde*, to dominate the space and use it as a site of fashionable display and performative spectacle. The period that followed, 1786 to 1810, was characterised by slowly declining ticket prices, changing ticketing practices, and shifts in advertising that all reflected the move to wider commercialisation and presence of the middling sorts.

While these characteristics are significant components of the masquerade and necessary to establish the framework and chronology of this Element, it is equally important to understand the way the term 'masquerade' was used within the eighteenth century. Popular forms of assembly, like the ridotto, fête, ball, and masquerade, each involved a varied combination of similar components – musical performance, dance, and/or elaborate décor. The masquerade, however, maintained a unique position and clear identity within Georgian leisure culture through its namesake: the mask and habit.[6] This was a central defining feature of the entertainment, as was the necessity of a ticket for entry and the ceremonial

---

[5] Kobza, 'Dazzling or Fantastically Dull', 169–70. Opera tickets were seldom higher than half a guinea for a box, five shillings for the pit, and 2s 6d for the gallery. There were special ticket prices for some operas, including galas and opening nights when prices might rise; however, these were considered 'regular' rates. In his work on Vauxhall, David Hunter has cited admission to Vauxhall and Ranelagh Gardens costing between one and two shillings, placing these leisure sites significantly lower than the price of a masquerade ticket. David Hunter, 'Rode the 12,000? Counting Coaches, People and Errors En Route to the Rehearsal of Handel's *Music for the Royal Fireworks* at Spring Gardens, Vauxhall in 1749', *The London Journal* 37, no. 1 (March 2012): 13–26, 16; *Morning Chronicle and London Advertiser*, 15 May 1777; *Public Advertiser*, 24 May 1777.

[6] John Kersey, in *A new English dictionary* (London: Robert Knaplock at Bishop's Head, 1713); Nathan Bailey, in *Dictionarium Britannicum* (2nd ed., London: T. Cox, 1730); Samuel Johnson, in *Johnson's Dictionary of the English Language in Minature* (8th ed., London: Lee and Hurst, 1797).

unmasking. Ticketing aided in regulating admittance, reinforcing the masquerade's exclusive nature, while concluding the evening with a grand unmasking held participants accountable for their behaviour throughout the entertainment. These main features were present in masquerades throughout the century, making it an identifiable and familiar leisure experience.[7]

1.2 Roots of the Domino

The Venetian domino has received considerable attention in both dress history and cultural history, surfacing in the work of Aileen Ribeiro, Terry Castle, and John Eglin among others. Their work defines the function and physical construction of this classic Venetian garment and analyses the domino within the context of *carnavale*.[8] Ribeiro and Castle draw important connections between this Italian piece and its presence and reputation in British masquerade spaces. Re-examining these cultural roots provides a foundation that allows for a closer comparison of the Italian and British iterations. Studying the domino in both places highlights that while the British domino took inspiration from its Venetian counterpart, it underwent a series of small evolutions that impacted its function and reputation in British masquerade spaces throughout the eighteenth century.

The domino originated in Venice, where it functioned predominately as a disguise to protect elite identity. It was most commonly associated with the pre-Lenten festivities of *carnavale* when public spaces were open to the rich and plebeians alike. From the month of December through to mid-February, the domino was worn in the streets by people from various ranks and occupations, which increased its presence in the public eye and created scenes filled with black cloaks and white masks. Although the domino appeared in the highest numbers during *carnavale*, it had multiple functions and was also worn during ceremonies of state and within the walls public of gaming houses.[9] This exhibits the domino's continued use throughout the year and highlights that the garment was not confined to a singular space, entertainment, or event. The domino's non-*carnavale* functions do, however, show that it was tied to a singular rank of people – the elite.[10]

---

[7] Kobza, 'Dazzling or Fantastically Dull', 164.

[8] Ribeiro, *The Dress Worn at Masquerades in England*; Ribeiro, *Dress in Eighteenth-Century Europe*; Castle, *Masquerade and Civilization*; Eglin, *Venice Transfigured*.

[9] Castle, *Masquerade and Civilization*, 58–9; Ribeiro, *Dress in Eighteenth-Century Europe*, 245–7; Eglin, *Venice Transfigured*, 59–61; Peter Burke, *Popular Culture in Early Modern Europe* (London: Harper and Row: 1978).

[10] Ribeiro, *Dress in Eighteenth-Century Europe*, 247.

The domino outfit consisted of several characteristic pieces: a black cloak, a mask, a tricorn hat, and an optional veil for added concealment.[11] The cloak itself was often identified as the defining component of the ensemble and its colour the cause of censure and commentary. Travellers on the Grand Tour and foreign ambassadors often 'noted the gravity of Venetians even during their prolonged Carnival season, and those … depicted in black domino and white mask seem oddly dour, as they did to the traveller who remarked on the monotony and seemingly inappropriate solemnity of the ubiquitous domino'.[12] Each piece hid a particular part or parts of the body: the cloak covered the torso and legs, the mask concealed the face, the hat hid the top of the head and hair, and the veil kept the neck, head, and mouth out of sight. This is seen in many of Pietro Longhi's paintings, which depict Venetians in a range of places and scenes in domino dress. Longhi's work depicts domino cloaks in multiple lengths and shows how the mask, veil, and hat worked together to cover the face and head. Ribeiro identified these differences in cloak styles, explaining that 'occasionally the short net or lace cloak, the *mantellina*' was used in place of the full-length option, being 'light and floating' in nature.[13]

With black dominos as the uniform of Venetians (and the elite in particular), foreign visitors partaking in *carnavale* were left to dress in more colourful variations. The bright garments of ambassadors, dignitaries, and those on the Grand Tour made foreigners easier to identify and brought pops of colour into an otherwise dark scene. Colour was not the only potential indicator of identity – differences in mask styles could betray gender and varying lengths in cloaks could reveal expensive dress that was indicative of wealth and status. The black *moretta* mask was part of a woman's traditional domino dress, though it could also be worn on its own. Its round shape covered only and exactly the area of the face – eyes, nose, and mouth. A bead or button held in the wearer's mouth kept the mask on the face, disguising the face and incapacitating the voice as points of identification. The *bauta* mask was characteristic of men's domino dress and opposite to the *moretta* in colour, shape, and application (Figure 1). Its white colour stood out from the black cloak, veil, and hat of the domino, unlike the *moretta*, and it was attached by tying a string around the head, leaving the mouth unencumbered. The rough square shape of the mask covered the eyes and nose, but drew away from the mouth and chin to accommodate eating, drinking, and speaking. In addition, the anonymity of the domino could have been enhanced through the addition of a piece of silk or lace, 'placed on the head and drawn

---

[11] Ribeiro, *Dress in Eighteenth-Century Europe*, 246–7.   [12] Eglin, *Venice Transfigured*, 56.
[13] Ribeiro, *Dress in Eighteenth-Century Europe*, 247.

Figure 1 Venetian *bauta* mask, author's collection

across the lower jaw'.[14] When worn together, these main components – black cloak, veil, *moretta* or *bauta* mask, and hat – physically defined the Venetian domino costume and made it a distinct and recognisable form of disguise across Europe. Outside of Italy, the Venetian domino could be worn in pre-Lenten festivities but was most prevalent in leisure spaces of elite sociability that occurred throughout the year, such as masquerades and fancy dress parties. Its consistent presence at court masquerades in France, Germany, and Sweden pointed to widespread recognition and use among the upper ranks and nobility. Dressing in the Venetian domino exhibited knowledge of elite Venetian culture while also signalling ties to or experiences of the Grand Tour. The domino had comparable popularity within British masquerade culture; however, due to the commercial nature of the entertainment, the domino grew into various iterations and embodied a range of meanings that were dependent on its acquisition, materiality, wearer, and geographical context.

1.3 The British Domino

As the domino moved from Venice to London and into other metropoles of Britain, its original function and key characteristics evolved to cater to the commercial masquerade experience. These changes resulted in three defining aspects of the British domino that reflected its Venetian roots while establishing it as a crucial but increasingly contentious symbol of the masquerade. This is exhibited through changes to its defining physical components, range of

---

[14] Ribeiro, *Dress in Eighteenth-Century Europe*, 246–7; Meghan Kobza, 'The Habit of Habits: Material Culture and the Eighteenth-Century London Masquerade', *Studies in Eighteenth-Century Culture* 50, no. 1 (2021): 269–70.

availability, and limited geographical use. Beginning with a brief overview of these three qualities provides a foundational working knowledge of the domino that will be useful when moving into more detailed analyses of the habit in subsequent sections.

The British domino was not unlike the Venetian equivalent in that it consisted of a draping cloak, mask, and head covering. In both locations, these components allowed the wearer to determine the level of concealment their habit provided and remain anonymous or recognisable. Wearers could decide on their style of mask independent of their gender and if they would cover their head with a hat, the attached hood, or leave it bare. Similarly, it was up to the wearer to select the colour, any embellishments, and the length of the cloak. British iterations could vary from this style and often mixed and matched the domino cloak with the *bauta* or an eye mask, and/or the tricorn hat. The veil, however, was one component the British left in Venice. Rather than use the veil as an additional face and head covering, the British domino mask used a smaller piece of fabric attached to the bottom of the mask as a means to conceal the mouth and jaw. This is evidenced in an existing masquerade mask and in multiple contemporary British prints spanning the eighteenth century (Figures 2, 3, and 4). In each image the mask worn with the domino is reminiscent of the structure and shape of the *bauta* but depends on a small swatch of fabric to cover the lower half of the face rather than the Venetian veil. This made it easier to eat and breathe within the often hot rooms of masquerade venues.

The distinction between a 'regular' and Venetian style domino appears across several contemporary masquerade experiences, pointing to the British version being recognised as a version all its own. A masquerade warehouse

Figure 2 Silk and tarlatan masquerade mask, c.1780–90, Museum of London

Figure 3 'An Epistle to Miss – &c. &c.' 1749, courtesy of the Lewis Walpole Library, Yale University

auction list distinguished between the types of domino available, labelling some as simply 'domino' and others as a 'bahoote [bauta] domino' or 'Venetian domino', though there is little detail to differentiate one from another.[15] This variety in domino style also appeared in personal accounts, indicating a clear

---

[15] Spellings include bauta, bahoote, and bahute.

Figure 4 Daniel Dodd, *Charles Revelling at a Masquerade*, c.1770–80, courtesy of the Lewis Walpole Library, Yale University

difference, but similarly lacked clarification in what qualified a domino as *bauta* or 'Venetian'. The Duchess of Northumberland identified varying styles of domino at a masquerade in 1768, using 'Venetian' and 'bahute' to distinguish this particular type from just a 'domino'.[16] Her use of 'bahute' and 'Venetian' point to these labelled dominos as resembling the classic *bauta* mask and black cloak associated with the Venetian practices of wearing the ambiguous disguise and highlight an implied difference between these and the expected British version.

Another important identifying characteristic of the British domino was its commercial availability and the choice to wear black or a more colourful option, regardless of national affiliation. As previously discussed, black dominos were limited to use by Venetians, making them an exclusionary garment and making visitors dress in a non-black garment. While the coloured dress code of Venice did not formally apply to British masquerades, the accessibility of the domino was heavily dictated by financial limitations. In theory, dominos were available to everyone – hopeful masqueraders could choose to borrow or purchase a domino and acquire one without needing to rely on credit or social status. However, the price of acquisition when combined with the cost of a masquerade ticket would have barred the majority of the population from even infrequent attendance. During the height of masquerade culture (1762–85), admittance to the top three masquerade venues, Carlisle House in Soho Square, King's Theatre, or the Pantheon, would have cost an average of two guineas and

---

[16] Diaries of Elizabeth Percy, Duchess of Northumberland, MSS 121/5a, 25, the archives of the Duke of Northumberland, Alnwick Castle.

seven shillings, which did not include the expense of a costume and transportation. Even at in its most basic form, a domino might run half a guinea (10s 6d), but the *Middlesex Journal* shows that even this low price was unlikely, estimating 'the price of all the various dresses at three guineas each', which was based on 'the money demanded at Tavistock-street for the use only of a domino'.[17] Anyone interested in joining the masquerade scene would, at minimum, have to surrender a total of three and a half guineas.[18] Even as the masquerade moved to wider trends in commercialisation, including the ability to hire a domino on site, the price range of a domino (5s to £4) and average masquerade ticket (16s) left the lowest rate of attendance at one guinea. This would have been 219 per cent of an average middling household's weekly disposable income, highlighting the rarity of attendance for those within this social category.[19] These prices alone were considerable financial barriers, keeping the masquerade, and in many instances the domino, out of reach for the middling ranks and making it a disguise of the elite rather than the wider public.

The last important feature of the domino relates to its geographic footprint and singular use as a masquerade costume. As Ribeiro and Eglin have both explained, the Venetian domino was worn throughout the year – appearing in the streets during *carnavale* festivities and in courts of law, public gaming houses, and other ceremonies of state outside of the months of *carnavale*.[20] The British domino did not hold this same multifunctional purpose and was only allowed within the confines of masquerade spaces and viewing parties. This narrowed its cultural meaning from a garment that doubly served as a formal way to protect identity and ceremonial dress for pre-Lenten festivities to a commercial costume. Outside of the masquerade the domino had no use unless it was refashioned into another garment. Its singular purpose emphasised its dependency on the masquerade and made it a key symbol of the masquerade in wider leisure and popular culture.

---

[17] 5–7 May 1772.

[18] Roughly 96 per cent of the population could not afford to attend the masquerade at this price point. Kobza, 'Dazzling or Fantastically Dull', 166–8, 70–1. See also Robert D. Hume, 'The Value of Money in Eighteenth-Century England: Incomes, Prices, Buying Power – and Some Problmes in Cultural Economics', *Huntington Library Quarterly* 77, no. 4 (2015): 373–416; Peter Earle, 'The Middling Sort in London', in *The Middling Sort of People: Culture, Society, and Politics in England, 1550–1800*, ed. Christopher Brooks and Johnathan Barry (London: Macmillan, 1994), 141–58.

[19] This is based on McKendrick's estimate of an annual disposable income of £25 for middling households in 1770 in 'The Commercialization of Fashion', 29. See Table 4 in Kobza, 'Dazzling or Fantastically Dull', 171, for a further price comparison of masquerade ticket prices in relation to household incomes.

[20] Eglin, *Venice Transfigured*, 59–60; Ribeiro, *Dress in Eighteenth-Century Europe*.

2 Three Dominos

This section engages with Riello's practice of drawing history 'from things' and therefore uses three physical dominos as the main pieces of evidence. This methodology takes a material culture approach and applies an in-depth analysis to objects, treating them as primary sources (much in the same way historians use manuscripts, diaries, or other sources).[21] The work of Lorna Weatherill, Amanda Vickery, Zara Anishanslin, and Kimberly Alexander, among others, emphasises the importance of including material culture in historical research and shows that objects have the power to shape existing historical narratives and create new avenues of research.[22] Like Karen Harvey's work on the trouser and men's legs, this section depends on a range of sources to reconsider the materiality and physicality of the domino and understand how it was worn.[23] A close study of three existing dominos in the collections of the Victoria and Albert Museum, the Metropolitan Museum of Art (the Met), and the Museum of London answers questions about the domino as a British masquerade habit and provides insight into its construction and materiality as well as what it allowed wearers to hide or reveal. These samples were the only three I was able to find for material analysis in readily accessible collections, pointing to its ephemeral nature and ability to be made into other garments. The dominos exhibit a range in colour and variety of styles, indicating it was both distinct and changeable. It is important to recognise that this study is limited by the small number of surviving objects, particularly when thinking about the domino within a larger context; however, contemporary imagery, personal accounts, and a masquerade warehouse's inventory are used to supplement this material evidence. This combination of sources contributes additional essential perspectives on masquerade praxis, the way dominos were adapted to British masquerade spaces, and why this costume appealed to so many masqueraders.

---

[21] Jules David Prown, 'Mind in Matter: An Introduction to Material Culture Theory and Method', *Winterthur Portfolio*, 17, no. 1 (1982); Riello, 'Things that Shape History: Material Culture and Historical Narratives', 28.

[22] Lorna Weatherill, *Consumer Behaviour and Material Culture in Britain, 1660–1760*, 2nd ed. (London: Routledge, 1996); Amanda Vickery, *Gender, Taste, and Material Culture in Britain and North America 1700–1830*; Giorgio Riello and Anne Gerritsen, eds. *Writing Material Culture* (London: Bloomsbury Academic, 2015); Anishanslin, *Portrait of a Woman in Silk*; Kimberly S. Alexander, *Treasures Afoot: Shoes Stories from the Georgian Era* (Baltimore: Johns Hopkins University Press, 2018); Chloe Wigston Smith and Serena Dyer, eds., *Material Literacy in Eighteenth-Century Britain: A Nation of Makers* (London: Bloomsbury, 2020); Serena Dyer, 'State of the Field: Material Culture', *History* 106, no. 370 (2021): 282–92.

[23] Karen Harvey, 'Men of Parts: Masculine Embodiment and the Male Leg in Eighteenth-Century England', *Journal of British Studies* 54, October (2015): 800–1.

2.1 Object Descriptions

The Pink Domino

This Element begins with a pink women's domino, housed within the Textiles and Fashion Collection at the Victoria and Albert Museum (Figure 5). This domino was made in London between 1765 and 1770 and underwent a few alterations around 1775. It measures 175 cm from the bottom hem to the top of the hood along the centre line. The fabric used is pink lustring, or lutestring, which was a light, shiny silk.[24] It is a long robe with a frontal opening, an attached cape that drapes over the shoulders, and a hood. The collar and cuffed sleeves have button fasteners to secure the garment and hold it in place around the neck and wrists respectively. The body features pinked and ruched scalloped embellishments that trim the edge of the cape, sleeves, and hood and form a serpentine curve along the front panels of the garment.[25] There are also several flowers tacked to the front panels of the garment, adding texture and flare.

Figure 5 Pink silk domino, c.1765–70 ©Victoria and Albert Museum, London

---

[24] Amanda Vickery, 'Mutton Dressed as Lamb? Fashioning Age in Georgian England', *Journal of British Studies* 52, no. 4 (2013): 882.

[25] Janet Arnold, 'A Pink Domino c.1760–70 at the Victoria and Albert Museum', Victoria and Albert Museum, 2009, https://collections.vam.ac.uk/item/O363441/domino-unknown/.

The White Domino

The second domino, housed in the Costume Institute collection at the Met, is made of white silk damask with a light silk lining on the interior and wool batting along the bottom hem (Figure 6). It was made in London during the eighteenth century and measures 146 cm from the base of the hem to the top of the hood along the front midline. The increasing popularity of both silk damask and the domino costume during the second half of the century could place the creation of this piece sometime around 1760 or 1770. This domino is a mid- to full-length hooded cloak (depending on the height of the wearer) with a frontal opening and shows possible signs of closure by two separate fasteners on the left side under the hood. There are no sleeves, but rather an opening on either side of the garment for each arm to pass through. The exterior and interior fabrics have both been cut in the shape of long oval holes and some of the excess material is pulled through, folded over, and sewn down to provide a finished edge all the way around. Pleats help create the shape of the attached hood and bring it to a close in the back just above the neckline. The shoulders also have one pleat each, which, like those in the hood, would allow the wearer to make alterations as necessary. The shattering along the neckline and creases (and visible conservation treatments) are evidence that this domino was worn often throughout its eighteenth-century life.[26]

Figure 6 White silk domino, c.1770, the Met

---

[26] Marci Morimoto, 'White Domino', email, 2021.

The Black Domino

The last of the dominos is in the collections of the Museum of London and is identified as being made between 1770 and 1790 (Figure 7). It is a loose robe of black silk measuring 136 cm from the top of the neckline to the bottom hem and is characterised by a frontal opening, pleated sleeves, draping oversleeves, and a Vandyke collar. Pinked, ruched trim runs along the sleeve cuffs, collar, and front hem, adding texture and embellishing the garment. The absence of a hood in this instance appears intentional; there are no alterations made around the collar to suggest its potential addition or removal, and the collar itself is one of the domino's key embellished features. The collar can be secured by a tie closure while each sleeve has a drawstring to open or close the space around the wrist.[27] Draping sleeves and oversleeves, like those seen here, were characteristic of the standard domino and portrayed in several contemporary images (Figures 3 and 8). This wide-mouthed construction would allow the wearer to put on or remove their domino with relative ease and made the domino more readily transferrable if used by bodies of varying sizes and with underclothes of differing styles.

Figure 7 Black silk domino, c.1760, Museum of London

---

[27] Item description of Black Silk Domino, 2000, 70.59/1, Museum of London.

2.2 Materiality

Overarching similarities link the three garments together, while the unique material features and physical characteristics of each shed new light on who might have worn the domino, how it was worn, and why it remained a consistent costume choice for the British masquerade. Each of the dominos are identified as being made, and in some cases altered, in London during the second half of the eighteenth century.[28] This dates their creations to London's peak masquerade period (1762–85), which experienced the highest prices in ticketing and highest prevalence of masquerades in commercial venues. The overlapping periodisation of these three surviving dominos speaks to an increase in the production of domino habits and a subsequent increase in the lifespan of the garment – extending beyond that of an active masquerade habit and transitioning into a collectible costume. The existence of these dominos likewise suggests more frequent use of this type of habit among masquerade participants. When looking at the dominos as a joint body of evidence, there are two central themes that come forward: materiality (fabric, colour, embellishments) and physicality (stitching, alterations, bodily covering capabilities). Examining the above dominos across these categorisations provides new evidence of the habit's multifaceted function and indicates that its customisable nature and ease of wear strongly appealed to the elite. Contemporary newspaper reports and the observations and experiences of masquerade participants, such as Horace Walpole, the Duchess of Northumberland, and Frances Burney, supplement the evidence embodied in the extant garments and contribute to a more comprehensive understanding of the domino's function and place within the British masquerade scene.

Fabric

The material nature of any garment is first and foremost defined by the fabric from which it was made. Each of the above dominos was constructed from silk, which was used to form the main body of the habit as well as any additional features or embellishments. This significant aspect of the dominos' design links the three together and establishes expectations of a domino's shiny visual appearance. The silk used in the pink and black dominos is lustring, named so for its lustrous shine, and was a popular fabric choice for elite formal dress and footwear worn at court.[29] Lustring has been identified as one of the most important materials of the

---

[28] Arnold, 'A Pink Domino'; 'Domino: 18th Century' (Silk), The Met, www.metmuseum.org/art/collection/search/90514; Mask & Cloak, 70.59, Dress and Textiles, Museum of London.

[29] Joanna Marschner and Nigel Arch, *Splendour at Court: Dressing for Royal Occassions since 1700* (London: Unwin Hyman, 1987), 40–1; Ribeiro, *Dress in Eighteenth-Century Europe*; Vickery, 'Mutton Dressed as Lamb', 882; Anishanslin, *Portrait of a Woman in Silk*, 148–51.

eighteenth century and was a standard dress material, ranging in price from 5s to 15s per yard. The white domino is made of damask silk, which was patterned and produced a similar shine to lustring. Like lustring, damasks were widely used but often higher priced at 12s to 15s per yard.[30] The cost of these fabrics alone points to elite use, as several yards were used to construct the dominos and the added expense of labour would have brought the overall price into a range of one to two guineas. Both types of silk were often enhanced with gold or silver thread or trim to complement their natural sheen and draw attention to the wearer and display their status. This process would have led to a further increase in price, often doubling the cost of fabric and bringing the domino to nearly £4.[31] In addition to its shine, the woven nature of silk damask made it inherently heavier and harder-wearing than lustring while still providing its wearer with a lustrous garment. This made silk damask ideal for dresses and waist-coats alike, while its reversibility allowed owners to turn the material inside out and reuse it when existing pieces of clothing became worn.[32] The interior lining of the white domino would have effectively protected the backside of the silk damask and provided the wearer the possibility to use it again later if needed. In his correspondence, Horace Walpole suggests this as an option, recommending his friend send for his tailor immediately 'to get you a sober purple domino as I have done, and it will make you a couple of summer waistcoats'.[33] Deconstructing and reusing the fabric of a domino in this way points to the need for durable and fashionable material, as it would continue to represent the wearer's taste and status beyond the walls of the masquerade.

Colour

Although they are connected by silk and shine, the three dominos appear more distinct than similar when considering their colour and overall style. Of these features, colour is the first to grab the eye and helps distinguish the habits from each other – the pink domino, the white domino, the black domino. The production and wearing of colourful dominos, like the rose-pink or white options, came from elite experiences of the Grand Tour where foreigners were obligated to dress in more colourful options. Venetians themselves were entitled to wear the classic black, which functioned both at masquerades and as identity-obscuring streetwear

[30] Natalie Rothstein, *Silk Designs of the Eighteenth Century In the Collection of the Victoria and Albert Museum, London with a Complete Catalogue* (London: Bulfinch Press, 1990), 290–1, 86.

[31] Rothstein, *Silk Designs of the Eighteenth Century*, 23.

[32] Rothstein, *Silk Designs of the Eighteenth Century*, 286; Anishanslin, *Portrait of a Woman in Silk*, 118–19, 48–51.

[33] Horace Walpole, 'Letter to Horace Mann', 28 May 1763, *The Yale Edition of Horace Walpole's Correspondence*, vol. 40 (New Haven: Yale University Press, 1937–83), 284.

throughout the year. While black dominos were worn at British masquerades, neither they nor their more colourful counterparts were part of a sumptuary code, but rather were worn based on preference or availability. In a letter to his brother, James Brudenell described his last-minute domino as *beautiful*, being 'straw coloured trimed with Purple'.[34] Brudenell's status as a high-ranking member of the elite did not direct him to choose black, but rather an option he found attractive and reflective of his taste. The Duchess of Northumberland recalled a few multicol-oured dominos in her diary: 'Lord Granby had a white Domino trimm'd with Gold. Lord Orford the same trimm'd with Gold & Scarlet' while Major Clements was in 'a very pretty white Domino trimm'd with Maron Black & Gold'.[35] Her account of a masquerade in 1769 similarly noted the Duchess of Bolton in a black domino and the Duke of Gloucester wearing a scarlet domino trimmed with silver.[36] Frances Burney likewise noted the colour and trimming of an acquaintance, recording 'Miss Strange had a White sattin Domino trimed with Blue.'[37]

Colours also circulated through newspaper reports and contemporary literature describing masquerade scenes, the former listing specific individuals and the shade they wore with the latter using colour as a form of character identification. The *Morning Herald and Daily Advertiser* described the Prince of Wales and eighteen named members of the nobility wearing black dominos, while the Duke of Cumberland was dressed in light blue.[38] Green, grey, orange, and rose also surfaced in masquerade news, expanding the spectrum of colours beyond the ever popular and overworn black.[39] The range in colours across these sources demon-strates that dominos could be made in one colour, such as the pink and white iterations or Walpole's purple selection, or many colours, like Brudenell's straw trimmed with purple. Wearing a non-black domino, while still considered a dull costume, was looked upon more favourably than sporting the black. One news-paper shared that despite an overwhelming presence of dominos at the Pantheon masquerade, 'a great variety of colours prevailed' and they 'produced an effect very preferable to the *mezzotinto* appearance of *uniform* black'.[40] Not only could

---

[34] James Brudenell, later Lord Brudenell and Lord Cardigan, to his brother Thomas Brudenell, 4th Earl of Ailesbury, 26 May 1763, letter, MSS 9/35/316, Wiltshire and Swindon Archives, Chippenham, England.

[35] Diaries of Elizabeth Percy, Duchess of Northumberland, MSS 121/5a, 25, June 1763, the archives of the Duke of Northumberland, Alnwick Castle.

[36] Diaries of Elizabeth Percy, Duchess of Northumberland, MSS 121/31, 20, 1 June 1769, the archives of the Duke of Northumberland, Alnwick Castle.

[37] Frances Burney journal entry 1770, *The Early Journals and Letters of Fanny Burney. Vol.1, 1768–1773*, ed. Lars E. Troide (Oxford: Clarendon, 1988), 101.

[38] *Morning Herald and Daily Advertiser*, 11 June 1781.

[39] *General Evening Post*, 15–17 May 1770; *St. James's Chronicle or the British Evening Post*, 11–13 May 1780;

[40] *Morning Herald*, 30 January 1782.

the array of single and multicolour options shift the palette away from the blacks of *carnavale*, it allowed masquerade participants to customise their dominos and display their tastes through dress. These qualities were echoed in popular literature with coloured dominos offering authors ways to identify notable 'disguised' characters during masquerade scenes whose identities would later be revealed. Both Henry Fielding and Frances Burney referred to key characters using colour within their climactic masquerade scenes; Fielding relied on a blue domino to single out the then-disguised Mrs James while Burney used a white domino to introduce and distinguish the then-unknown but later significant character of Mr Mortimer Delvile.

Embellishments

Trim and embellishments were equally significant features that could be tailored to reflect individual status and fashionability. Each of the three dominos shows how various combinations of these options were indicative of the wearer's rank and taste, upending the habit's responsibility to conceal identity. The pink and black dominos have a number of overlapping similarities in this respect. The collars, sleeve cuffs, oversleeves, and front opening seams are trimmed with extra fabric that has been ruched and pink'd along the edges. These details, plus the addition of serpentine ruching and flowers along the front panels of the pink domino, would have increased the cost of each garment. Additional fabric was required for the draping oversleeves and trim, and skilled labour was crucial to attach trim and flowers in a particular pattern, which would bring the price of these dominos into the higher end of the costume marketplace, setting the minimum price of these or similar dominos at two to three guineas (much above the half guinea mentioned earlier) and limiting their use to the upper ranks.[41] Though different to the visible exterior trim on the pink and black dominos, the interior lining and wool batting of the white domino would also have incurred labour and fabric expenses, bringing it in line with the upper price range of the domino market.

Upgrades of this nature, as well as the use of silk to make the domino, are clear signs of material wealth, status, and taste, as the Duchess of Northumberland continually reminds us in her diaries. The gold and silver trimming mentioned in her earlier masquerade reports are used on four of the five habits and offered an additional glistening component that duly would have flashed the wearer's wealth and increased the cost of the domino to nearly double.[42] Her appreciation of these dominos provides a stark contrast to her thoughts on the dress of the royal family. Much to her disapproval, 'the Queens

---

[41] Kobza, 'The Habit of Habits', 274–5.
[42] Rothstein, *Silk Designs of the Eighteenth Century*, 23.

two Brothers were by much the two shabbiest figures there, they were in plain Lutestring Domino's (which did not even appear to be clean) with each a Ribbon scantilly set round their Cape without any other Trimming whatever'.[43] This critique of the princes' dominos shows an unspoken expectation that masquerade participants should dress according to rank, regardless of whether they were well disguised or not. Her particular comments on the tattered ribbon and absence of trimming emphasise the weight material details held in acting as key identifiers of status, overriding the domino's function as a form of concealment. A portrait of Francis Osborne, the fifth Duke of Leeds, provides visual evidence of these expectations and illustrates the types of trim the upper ranks might use (Figure 8). His gleaming white domino has a cape and draping sleeves, both of which have scalloped edges and are trimmed in gold and flowers. The central opening is likewise embellished with gold – a clear symbol of his wealth that, captured on canvas, would outlast the life of his domino. Masquerade warehouse advertisements likewise conveyed these types of embellishments, trimmings, and other fashionable add-ons were meant for elite use. Descriptions of recently acquired stock were addressed to the 'Nobility and Gentry', with dominos regularly described as available in all colours and 'trimm'd and embellish'd in a polite Taste'.[44] At the very least, the added expense of trim, oversleeves, pinking, lining, or any combination of four would have functioned as points of recognition and signalled wear by members of the upper ranks who could afford upgrades of this nature.

Figure 8 Benjamin West, *Francis Osborne, 5th Duke of Leeds*, c.1769
© National Portrait Gallery, London

---

[43] Duchess of Northumberland, MSS 121/31a, 1 June 1769, 120.
[44] *General Advertiser*, 7 February 1750.

Hoods

The hoods of the pink and white dominos and Vandyke collar of the black domino are contrasting, significant material features that further indicate how customisation made the domino ideal for use among the upper ranks. The hoods attached to the collars of both the pink and white dominos are of a similar construction, formed by pleats that are sewn down at the back of the hood and just above the collar. Shattering along the interior seams of the hood and along the collar provide clear signs of wear in the white domino.[45] Telling alterations on the pink domino reveal a similar amount of use – the collar and hood show signs of unpicking and restitching, while a closer examination of the hood reveals two panels that were added to enlarge its volume capacity. These adjustments indicate that it was used to cover the head and accompanying wig rather than serving as a purely decorative feature.[46] Extending the height of the hood to accommodate the popular tall wigs of the mid-1770s and the noticeable shattering inside the white hood reinforce that hoods were actively worn as part of the domino and highlight that despite changes in fashionable trends, the purpose and manner of wearing this domino remained fairly consistent. Hooded dominos like these were one style of the habit and offered an all-inclusive but still customisable option for masquerade dress. The inclusion of a hood meant the wearer only needed to handle a mask and cloak, making this version of the domino more portable and even pocket-sized. Upon taking off his domino, Lord Peterborough 'rolled it up, and put it in his pocket' while other masquerade hopefuls were reported carrying 'a domino in their pocket' in order to quickly 'whip it on, and march into the supper rooms'.[47] The physical flexibility of the domino exhibited here highlights elite dependency on the habit as a convenient solution to avoid dressing in character and attend the masquerade without much forethought.

The absence of the hood on the black domino is equally as important as its presence on the pink and white habits. The missing hood removed an integral way to hide the wearer's hair and neck – physical clues that could be used jointly to discover identity. Knowing that their head would be bare, the wearer may have chosen to display a tall wig or sport a tricorn or other hat, not unlike a tall gentleman who 'wore his own Hair, with a plain Hat' with his pink domino.[48] Regardless of which option was worn, the collar created an implicit need for a separate head covering and an ancillary expense. Contemporary images of

---

[45] Morimoto email.   [46] Arnold, 'A Pink Domino'.
[47] *Morning Herald and Daily Advertiser*, 23 April 1782; *Morning Chronicle and London Advertiser*, 11 April 1785.
[48] *General Advertiser*, 16 April 1752.

dominos illustrate this version of the habit most frequently accompanied by a feathered or hat – the domino strewn on the chair in Figure 9 exhibits this clearly, as does the domino at the front right of Figure 10, while the few dominos in Figure 10 are identified by the cloak and feathered hat (front left) and just the feathered caps (along the back). Osborne's portrait showcases this design as well; he is wearing a stylised collar and cape with the accompanying feathered hat just behind his right shoulder. Masquerade warehouses also publicised this pairing, regularly listing feathered hats alongside dominos in their advertisements, suggesting the two were worn together with a mask to create the full

Figure 9 Carington Bowles, *The Prodigal Son Revelling with Harlots*, 1792, courtesy of the Lewis Walpole Library, Yale University

Figure 10 Giovani Antonio Canaletto, *View of the Rotundo House & Gardens at Ranelagh*, c.1759, author's collection

disguise.[49] Thomas's Warehouse is one of many that highlights this and the separate cost. The advertisement listed a 'great variety of dresses and dominos to be sold or let, at 10s. 6d. for the night' but with a 'Choice of hats and feathers' made available for an extra two to three shillings. This extra piece, when added with the price of the domino, raised the total cost of purchase to between twelve and eighteen shillings.[50] The need for a hat therefore normally incurred an additional expense, raising the price of even the most basic domino and bringing the masquerade habit into the financial realm of the upper sorts.

The sum cost of the domino was not the only indicator of elite wear; the Vandyke collar itself holds multiple layers of reference to elite culture. Vandyke costume was consistently worn in portraiture throughout the eighteenth century as a unique form of fancy dress and inspired detailed enhancements on court dress among the gentry and nobility.[51] Vandyke's influence within the artistic

---

[49] *Morning Post and Daily Advertiser*, 10 April 1777; *Morning Post and Daily Advertiser*, 12 April 1779.

[50] *Morning Post and Daily Advertiser*, 3 April 1780; *Morning Herald and Daily Advertiser*, 3 March 1783.

[51] References to Vandyke and portraiture-influenced dress are mentioned in *The Yale Edition of Horace Walpole's Correspondence*, vol. 17, 338, and the diaries of Elizabeth Percy, Duchess of Northumberland, MSS 121/31a, 28–30. For details of Vandyke dress worn and commissioned by

world led him and the style of dress within his works to become a favoured form of masquerade habit. This costume was a popular choice among the *beau monde* and was worn throughout the century. It allowed the wearer to display their taste and knowledge of the Old Masters through choice of dress and to exhibit their wealth through the accompanying sumptuous fabrics and jewels. The choice of adding a Vandyke collar to the domino was a nod to this fashion and solidifies connections between the wearer, classical portraiture, the masquerade, high culture, and taste. Both of these styles, hooded or elaborately collared, appear singularly in select satirical prints as symbols of the masquerade and were more sparingly depicted in wider masquerade scenes. Their appearances across material and visual sources shows how the British domino evolved from the Venetian roots into British iterations that were dependent on a cloak and a mask but left head coverings, embellishments, and mask style up to the discretion of the wearer.

Pleating

Upon closer examination, each of the three surviving dominos reveals additional clues about the ephemerality of this type of masquerade habit. The style of stitching throughout the object points to a need for ease of adjustment – the large stitches and pleats in the shoulders of the pink and black garments would have allowed the maker to tailor the size of the shoulders and length of the sleeves quickly.[52] These features suggest a domino had multiple wearers either from the same family or social network, or as it passed in and out of a warehouse. The ability to alter dominos upon receipt points to their frequently being rented or borrowed and passed across multiple wearers throughout their lifetimes. While buying a domino outright was always an option, as Walpole mentioned in his letter, renting and borrowing were also common means of acquiring this habit. Renting a domino entailed purchasing the costume for temporary use from a masquerade warehouse, while borrowing was done within one's family or social network and did not require a commercial transaction. Before describing his beautiful straw domino to his brother, Brudenell contemplated each form of acquisition and debated whether he had made the right choice in renting his domino:

> I hear … you would have lent me a clean Domino for the Masquerade at Richmond House. I wish I had known it sooner, for I am to pay 2 Guineas for the Hire of a Domino, which I have already bespoke; I should have been

---

George, Prince of Wales, and his brother Frederick, see Prince of Wales George, 'Letter to Frederick', in *The Correspondence of George Prince of Wales 1770–1821*, ed. Arthur Aspinall (London: Cassell, 1963), 57, 62. Ribeiro, *The Dress Worn at Masquerades in England*; Ribeiro, *Dress in Eighteenth-Century Europe*.

[52] Kobza, 'Habit of Habits', 272–6.

pleased to have spared that sum, but it is better than giving 4 Guineas & ½ to
have it entirely to myself: I shall be extreamly <u>beautiful</u>, a straw colour trimed
with Purple; what say you to that . . .[53]

After learning that his brother would have lent him one and saved
him the fee of two guineas, Brudenell reflects that borrowing a 'clean
Domino' from his brother would have been the best option. The Duchess
of Northumberland was also familiar with renting masquerade habits,
having rented 'a Black Domino & use of a Cloak' for £4 6s 6d with the purchase
of a 'Venetian Black Slk Mask' for 7s 6d.[54] The practice of renting a domino
from a warehouse was convenient – it could be done hours or days before the
masquerade and allowed maskers to continually change their habit so as not to be
caught in the same disguise twice (a fashion faux pas). The easily altered pleats
and rentals of dominos indicated there were limited emotional attachments made
to the habit, as it was widely viewed an invalid option after having served its
singular function for one night's entertainment.

2.3 Physicality and Movement

To understand the physicality of the domino, or the way it related to the body,
this section uses deduction and speculation to consider how it might have been
worn at masquerades. Conceptualising the praxis of wearing the domino
engages with the structural features of the existing samples (shape and length
of the garment, fasteners, and sleeves) and makes deductions from the way they
are draped on mannequins and how they are depicted in visual culture. While
each of the dominos was recognised and classified as a style of this particular
habit, there are clear differences that point to individual wearer's specifications
and how a number of options were available to customise. The surviving
dominos share a basic design that is carried through the construction of the
body – their resemblance to each other is visible in their robe-like structure and
draping nature. Each is characterised by a frontal opening that runs the length of
the garment and can be secured at the neckline. Though their lengths vary,
ranging from full (seen in the pink and black) to three-quarters (in the white), the
generous amount of fabric used in the width and length of the garments gives
them their enveloping properties and makes it clear that they were meant to offer
coverage through most of the body and fit over even the most voluminous of

---

[53] James Brudenell, *James Brudenell, later Lord Brudenell and Lord Cardigan, to his brother Thomas, 4th Earl of Ailesbury,* May 26, 1763, MSS 9/35/316, Wiltshire and Swindon Record Office.

[54] Elizabeth Percy, Duchess of Northumberland, '1744 Cloaths Account', MSS 121/174, the archives of the Duke of Northumberland.

dresses.[55] These front panels are anchored together via the collars, which exhibit different ways to fasten the domino; a button and loop secure the pink collar while the black is closed with a tie. The means to fasten the white domino is less clear, as there are only two small stitch marks under the hood on the left side of the collar, and none to match on the right. These hints suggest that the white either would have been left open entirely, closed solely at the neck, or lightly tacked to the wearer's evening attire. Small as they are, these details are significant because they are the only points of closure or attachment on the body of the garment, leaving the robe-like front the ability to flap open and expose the clothing underneath.

Customisable concealment extends from the body of the garment into the sleeves of the black and pink dominos, both of which also feature a range of ways to close. The sleeves on each domino offer the potential for fastening, presumably making dressing and undressing easier, as well as giving the masker the option to show or hide as much of their underdress as they desired. The pink domino has buttons on each sleeve cuff that are comparatively more anchored and defined points of closure than the adjustable drawstrings on the sleeves of the black. The absence of sleeves suggests that this part of the wearer's body would have been visible, as the arm openings would have sat around the wearer's elbows. Each of these options provided the wearer with a way to dress 'in disguise' while actually displaying their fashionable clothing and providing more visual points of recognition than maintaining anonymity. Placing the pink and black dominos on models helps conceptualise how they might offer the wearer a relatively high level of cover throughout the body (Figures 5 and 7). It is harder to imagine the extent to which the white would have done, as its fragile state makes it impossible to place on a mannequin – however, its similarity in structure to the pink and black suggests that it would have sat squarely on the wearer's shoulders and its draping qualities would have worked at least partially to conceal the clothing underneath. It is important to note that while modelling helps recreate the domino's relationship to the body, the mannequins and fabrics are static and do not fully reflect how the domino would have moved with its wearer through a masquerade space – being pulled tightly around the body as it left the carriage and entered the venue, opened to cool the wearer once inside the hot rooms, arranged just so to display a glittering dress underneath, or unintentionally tugged by other masquerade habits as the wearer moved about the space.

---

[55] When measured from top of the hood to the bottom front hem the pink domino is 67 in and the white is 57.5 in. The black domino is measured from top of collar to the bottom hem, running 53.5 in.

Figure 11 Close-up of bottom left; Giovani Antonio Canaletto, *View of the Rotundo House & Gardens at Ranelagh*, c.1759, author's collection

A small number of contemporary images provide additional perspective on how these dominos were worn, illustrating the varying coverage they might offer masqueraders. Like its Venetian predecessor, the domino could completely cover the body and make the wearer anonymous (despite newspaper reports and personal accounts proving otherwise). Popular prints such as 'An Epistle to Miss c. &c.' illustrate this high level of concealment, presenting the wearers as completely disguised under the folds of their habits. Despite their being caught in the midst of accosting Elizabeth Chudleigh (dressed in her controversial Iphigenia costume), their movement does not seem to impact the dominos' ability to hide their identities (Figure 3). Three additional portrayals of the domino supply further perspective on the changeable range of disguise the garment provided. The first image is taken from a larger masquerade scene at Ranelagh Gardens (Figure 13). The domino is in the bottom left of the etching and walking toward the edge of the frame. His black hat and cloak make him easily identifiable while two colours, blue and red, delineate the difference between his waistcoat and his habit – the waistcoat in red and cloak in blue. The cloak drapes open as he strolls down the path, doing little to hide him or his clothing and indicating that not all clad in a domino sought complete invisibility. The second depiction brings us back to the portrait of Francis Osborne, who

Figure 12 Carington Bowles, *The Chinese House, the Rotunda, and the Company in Masquerade at Ranelagh Gardens*, 1751, author's collection

Figure 13 Close-up of bottom left: Carington Bowles, *The Chinese House, the Rotunda, and the Company in Masquerade at Ranelagh Gardens*, 1751, author's collection

intentionally chose to don the habit in a portrait, which alone speaks to the relationship between the domino and the elite (Figure 8).[56] The white and gold domino he wears lies open at the neck, displaying a rich red suit underneath. Though the ribbon around the collar is untied, it is easy to see that even with a simple knot and bow, the front of the domino would have allowed Osborne to display his underdress through the front gap of the cloak. The wide, unstructured nature of the sleeves cover as much as they reveal and provide further evidence of his intention to wear the domino as a tool to emphasise his status rather than hide it. This domino strongly resembles the features of the black domino at the Museum of London, and seeing it draped on both a model and a person gives a strong impression as to how dominos might be used to showcase status in their seams and between floating hemlines.

The final image is taken from a series by Daniel Dodd that circulated in the 1770s and 1780s. It depicts a masquerade scene with an array of people wearing character or fancy dress with the titular character, Charles, positioned as the singular domino standing in the right foreground (Figure 4). The habit is an exceptionally close match to the pink domino, depicting a serpentine pattern across the front of the habit, and is embellished with trim along the edges of the collar, cape, and sleeve cuffs. It is secured at the top, like the pink or black would have been, and gapes open at the bottom showing buckles, shoes, and stockings (perhaps the leg of his breeches). The viewer sees Charles as he is entering the masquerade space, and his steps into the room are indicated through the placement of his feet and the exposure of his leg, showing that as he moved, the concealment of the domino shifted. The mixture of visual representations of these dominos proves that not all those who were domino-clad desired to completely hide themselves away beneath their habit.

In light of seeing how these habits and dominos in related contemporary images might offer concealment, it is equally as apparent that the physical features would have revealed as much as they hid.[57] The ability to tailor the dominos indicates this form of dress was a more transferable and temporary disguise used to cover everyday dress, unlike other masquerade habits that required full dress from head to toe. The signs of alterations and wear suggest that the domino functioned as a last-minute option for those who needed an immediate costume but lacked the time, creativity, or funds to

---

[56] Louise Lippincott, 'Expanding on Portraiture: The Market, the Public, and the Hierarchy of Genres in Eighteenth-Century Britain,', in *The Consumption of Culture 1600–1800: Image, Object, Text*, ed. Ann Bermingham and John Brewer (London: Routlege, 1995), 80–3; Brewer, *The Pleasures of the Imagination: English Culture in the Eighteenth Century*, 209.

[57] Kobza, 'The Habit of Habits', 275–8.

procure a more thoughtful masquerade habit. These qualities and characteristics point to elite use, which reinforce the masquerade's function as an elite
space of sociability.

3 The Domino as a Commodity

The masquerade warehouse often served as the first point of call for
those preparing to go to the masquerade. Warehouses offered the consumer
a variety of dress options: domino, character, or fancy dress; ready or custom
made; available to purchase or let; and priced between an average of seven
shillings and four guineas. These shops were an integral part of the masquerade
experience and remained key partners of the entertainment throughout the
century. The warehouse was likewise a central component of the domino's
life cycle and had a reciprocal relationship with this classic masquerade habit.
Examining the domino within the context of the masquerade warehouse not
only highlights the garment's function as a commodity but also shows how
changes in domino advertisements and pricing were reflective of shifts in the
affordability and accessibility of the masquerade itself. The domino therefore
provides new and important evidence of the prolonged exclusivity of the
masquerade despite wider trends in the commercialisation of leisure culture.

This section explores the relationship between the domino, the masquerade
warehouse, and the commercialisation of the masquerade using a combination
of geographical, quantitative, and qualitative analyses. It begins with a brief
analysis of the domino's starting point, the masquerade warehouse, and uses
three examples of the domino's transactional movement to consider how its
function as a loanable object impacted its dual nature as a commodity and
costume – ultimately showing it was an integral part of the masquerade industry.
Understanding the spatial origins for the habit and other masquerade dress sets
an important framework within which to examine the clientele and how proximity to both the buyer and masquerade venue reflected broader changes to the
entertainment and purpose of the domino. The section then moves from space to
text with a close reading of the descriptive language in warehouse advertisements, a surviving warehouse auction inventory, and manuscripts, each of
which point to the domino's value as a commodity and consistent feature within
the warehouse industry. Tracing key words across these sources shows that
verbal repetition and increasingly detailed descriptions underpinned contemporary understandings of the domino and contributed to a shared verbal landscape of masquerade culture that mirrored the masquerade's prolonged move to
accessibility through commercialisation. The section ends with an analysis of
the financial aspects of domino acquisition. Similar to the linguistic shifts,

advertised domino costs and the prices at which they were let and purchased offer additional evidence of their profitability and ability to fit a range of needs while simultaneously reflecting the delayed commercialisation of the masquerade.

The data used here is taken from newspaper advertisements, bills of sale, trade cards, a record from the Old Bailey, personal accounts, and an inventory list of a masquerade warehouse. The advertisements are drawn from 1,626 sources across 79 newspapers found in the Burney Collection. These examples provide an extensive range of data, including the names of the shops and sellers, their locations, the type of shop, and the goods they advertised. While this data supplies the foundation for quantitative and qualitative evidence about masquerade shops, the limitations of OCR required additional sources to supplement and cross-check this information.[58] The twenty-odd existing trade cards taken from collections in the British Museum, John Johnson collection, Westminster Archives, and regional record offices have been matched to nine newspaper businesses and provided three supplementary addresses of businesses as well as visual and descriptive detail about what was sold. The data taken from these sources was categorised chronologically, using the earliest newspaper advertisement to serve as a reference point for an estimated start of the business. Based on this data, the minimum number of distinct masquerade habit venues established throughout the eighteenth century was 121, with 49 new storefronts in the first half of the century and 72 in the second. The growing number of shops offered masquerade participants a range of locations where they could purchase or let their costumes. Though differing in name, these shops offered similar wares and regularly relied on the domino as a marketing tool and consistent part of their custom.

The value of the domino as a commodity is reinforced through a close examination of the linguistic shifts and financial changes in price listed in these advertisements. The number of papers and warehouses from the search in the Burney Collection provides a wide range of sources to examine consistencies and change over time. This data is complemented by the auction list of James Spilsbury's masquerade inventory, which supplies new information about costume types, material culture, and the masquerade warehouse industry more broadly. Itemised lots of habits and accessories, as well as the names of buyers and the accepted selling prices, reveal more details that provide the base for a quantitative analysis of the domino habit. Although this list is from only one of many masquerade warehouses of the period, Spilsbury's inventory can

---

[58] Trevor Muñoz, Simon Tanner, and Pich Hemy Ros, 'Measuring Mass Text Digitization Quality and Usefulness: Lessons Learned from Assessing the OCR Accuracy of the British Library's 19th Century Online Newspaper Archive', *D-Lib Magazine*, July/August 2009, www.dlib.org/dlib/july09/07munoz.html.

be seen as representative of its contemporaries due to overlapping similarities in advertisements, warehouse location, and the involvement of other warehouse owners in the auction.[59] Bringing together the data from Spilsbury's list and the analysis of advertisements allows for a nuanced examination of this habit type based in quantitative and qualitative evidence. This combination of evidence correlates to the height of masquerade culture and aligns with the material evidence the existing three dominos in Section 2 have introduced. Examining the domino within the context of the Spilsburys' business highlights the centrality of the domino to the masquerade experience both inside and outside the actual masquerade itself. This section, therefore, presents a new perspective on the domino in its role as a commodity and how its ties to the luxury market reflected the elite nature of the masquerade despite increasing trends commercialisation and accessibility within wider eighteenth-century leisure culture.

3.1 To and From the Warehouse

Using the data taken from newspapers and trade cards, it is possible to examine the shifts and consistencies of the shop locations in relation to fashionable shopping areas in London. This provides new perspectives on the social status and function of the masquerade, reinforcing its ties to the *beau monde* and elite leisure culture. Thinking about the spaces in which dominos were made and purchased contributes to their role within masquerade culture and gives them context outside of the masquerade itself, framing them as commodity rather than costume. The types of venues selling dominos and masquerade habits included small shops, coffeehouses, taverns, and warehouses. Coffeehouses and taverns operated as temporary masquerade shops throughout the first half of the century but discontinued their masquerade garment sales during the second half of the century as warehouses became the prime location for selling masquerade habits and related goods. This change in shop style indicated genteel and fashionable commercial underpinnings and a desire to cater to an elite clientele. It was common for warehouses to sell more than one type of product, including shirts, cloaks, and other linens, indicating involvement and ownership of the milliner trade.[60] This was the case for many of the warehouses offering masquerade goods. The adoption of masquerade goods within

---

[59] Timewell's and Thomas's Warehouses were both in business during the same time as Spilsbury and purchased several lots from the two-day auction. Together they bought 21 per cent of the auctioned lots (56 out of 266). *A Catalogue of the genuine, rich and very expensive Wardrobe Consisting of a Great Variety of Masquerade Dresses, the Property of Mr. Spilsbury*, auction by Mess. Christie and Ansell (Christie and Ansell's: London), 4 and 5 February 1779.

[60] Amy Louise Erickson, 'Eleanor Mosley and Other Milliners in the City of London Companies 1700–1750', *History Workshop Journal* 71 (Spring 2011): 159.

warehouses and specialty masquerade warehouses mirrors Maxine Berg's observation of the development of specialisation and segmentation within the market. The contemporary label of 'warehouse' indicated an availability of affordable items, often sold in bulk, which allowed for a rapid renewal of stock. From the 1760s onwards, this type of shop became increasingly associated with fashionable goods, as high product turnover allowed new fashions to become more rapidly available.[61] This was evidenced in the advertisements of many warehouses offering masquerade commodities. They listed their inventories as being filled with the newest and latest habits at the most reasonable prices:

> C. Kluht respectfully returns his sincere thanks to the Ladies and Gentlemen ... [and] takes the liberty to acquaint them, that his elegant and extensive Wardrobe of rich and comic character dresses, with a great variety of handsome dominos, is now opened for their inspection, at his Warehouse, No. 7, in Charles-street, Covent-garden ... where also are made and sold all sorts of mantua robes, sacks, gowns, habits, stys, &c. great variety of gold and silver gauzes, tissues, striped, and gold and silver sarsenets, tinsel laces, tassels, &c. Venetian and other masks.[62]

The increasing presence of masquerade commodities in milliner and haberdashery warehouses, as well as the establishment of masquerade warehouses themselves, indicated ties to the luxury market through linguistic cues. The choice to describe masquerade shops as warehouses, and of warehouses to advertise their selling of masquerade wares, indicated an exchange of association between the masquerade and the fashionable world of shopping, ultimately tying the masquerade to the *beau monde*. These ties were further made visible through the geographic locations of the warehouses and shops themselves. The choices of the owners and sellers to occupy spaces within high fashion and luxury areas reveals their intended customer base as well as an awareness of the masquerade's situation within the leisure culture of the elite. During the second half of the century, the concentration of newly established shops occupied Tavistock Street, the Strand, New Bond Street, and Oxford Street. These popular locations map directly onto Helen Berry's analysis of changes to London's central business districts, which identified luxury and fashionable retailers moving north and west during the second half of the century.[63] Berg further clarified

---

[61] Maxine Berg, *Luxury and Pleasure in Eighteenth-Century Britain* (Oxford: Oxford University Press, 2005), 265; Helen Berry, 'Polite Consumption: Shopping in Eighteenth-Century England', *Transactions of the Royal Historical Society* 12 (2002): 383.

[62] *Morning Post and Daily Advertiser*, 16 January 1777.

[63] Berg, *Luxury and Pleasure*, 261; Berry, 'Polite Consumption: Shopping in Eighteenth-Century England', 382. Lawrence Stone, 'The Residential Development of the West End of London in the Seventeenth Century', in *After the Reformation: Essays in Honor of J.H. Hexter*, ed. Barbara Malament (Manchester: 1980).

this, recognising that changes in corporate control and livery companies led to luxury trades congregating 'around the squares of Westminster' with a later shift to Piccadilly and St. James.[64] The presence of masquerade-related businesses continued into the 1790s, growing in concentration on Oxford Street with additional establishments in Piccadilly and St. James.

The predominance of masquerade shops in these areas makes it clear that the masquerade maintained an association with elite society and the luxury market, as they are concentrated in fashionable shopping areas. Setting up trade in these locations shows not only proprietor awareness of being included among fashionable spaces, but also customer recognition of these sites as selling fashionable products, of which the domino was included. The location of the warehouses within luxury shopping areas is important, as it sets the scene and tone of the shopping experience and origin of the domino on masquerade evenings. An additional geographical point deserving of analysis concerns the location of the habit-sellers in relation to elite residences and the masquerade venues themselves, which also illustrates the masquerade's commercial trajectory in relation to spectacle, exclusivity, and the eventual widening of consumer accessibility and participation. During the height of masquerade culture, the three main commercial masquerade venues in Westminster were within a mile of each other: King's Theatre, Carlisle House, the Pantheon. The residences of the nobility and gentry were similarly distributed within this radius, which was likewise sprinkled with masquerade warehouses throughout.[65] Having space and distance between the warehouse, site of preparation, and venue made the journey of the domino an extended experience as it moved from shop to residence to masquerade.

The experience of the Earl of Winterton is one example of the domino circulating within this area, having left a partial paper trail in its wake. An existing bill of sale from Pritchard's Warehouse, a popular masquerade dress supplier, recorded loaning a domino to the Earl of Winterton on 6 May 1772 (Figure 14). The date of the sale shows that Winterton completed the transaction and borrowed the domino the day preceding two large masquerades – one held at Carlisle House and the other at the Pantheon.[66] Both masquerades were continuously advertised and reported in several newspapers in the days leading up to and following their occurrence. While it is unclear which he attended, or if he indeed visited both, the decision to rent a domino the day prior to the event

---

[64] Berg, *Luxury and Pleasure*, 261.

[65] Amanda Vickery Hannah Greig, 'The Political Day in London, c. 1697–1834', *Past & Present* 252, no. 1 (2020): 110.

[66] *Middlesex Journal or Chronicle of Liberty*, 5–7 May 1772; *Morning Chronicle and London Advertiser*, 7 May 1772; *Craftsman or Say's Weekly Journal*, 9 May 1772.

Figure 14 Bill head of trade card of James Spilsbury, 1772 © The Trustees of the British Museum.

points to the domino as a choice of convenience rather than imaginative planning. Selecting and acquiring this habit within twenty-four hours of the masquerade did however leave enough time for the domino to move from Pritchard's on Tavistock Street to Winterton's house in Mayfair and to the masquerade before returning back to Pritchard's. As was customary, Winterton would have donned his habit before leaving his residence in order to arrive costumed at the entertainment, requiring him to wear the domino from his door to the venue. Travelling from home to the masquerade would have taken Winterton down main and side streets through the fashionable districts of London and consequently displayed him through the windows of either a carriage or a chair, making the domino an important component of his journey as it represented his status and taste. The cost of Winterton's domino, which was only hired for the use of one evening, was recorded at £3 3s and sits at the higher end of the price range. This price indicates his choice of domino would have been made of silk, complete with enough tasteful embellishments to reflect his rank, and resembled the style of either the pink or black domino discussed earlier. The domino's movement within this fashionable area shows how it shifted from commodity to costume and back to commodity again.

The proximity of these establishments suggests the masquerade and costuming experience were closely knit chronologically and geographically – the convenience of location allowed participants to purchase habits, put on their dress, and attend the masquerade all within the same evening. This is seen in a criminal case in the Old Bailey records, which provides more detail about the process of ordering a domino and the way it moved from warehouse to wearer.

This instance highlights an increasing awareness of the domino as a costume of convenience that was immediately available, mirroring the masquerade's widening commercial accessibility during the last decade of the century. The domino's movement and warehouse owner's actions show that the domino was considered an essential part of masquerade business and a profitable commodity, particularly if it was let. This case centres around the accusation of domino theft, which not only robbed the warehouse owner of the cost of making the domino, but also deprived them of future sales and profits from the domino's reusable nature as a frequently loaned habit.

The case began with an accusation against Thomas Lawrence for the theft of two black dominos, two masks, and a hat and feather from Thomas's Masquerade Warehouse.[67] A man acting on behalf of Lawrence visited the warehouse on Oxford Street around eight o'clock in the evening on April 7th, the evening of a masquerade at Ranelagh Gardens. He ordered dominos for Lawrence, specifying 'they must be good ones' and that they should be sent to a residence near Mayfair on Marylebone Street around nine o'clock. The quick turnaround time from order to delivery to masquerade venue indicates the domino's ready availability and ease of adjustment to fit whomever desired to borrow one, making it a habit of convenience. Judging by their listed price in the court records – masks at 2s, black silk dominos at 30s, and hat and feather at 30s – Thomas indeed selected 'good ones' for Lawrence and sent his servant, William Ward, to deliver them.

Thus the dominos started their journey, moving as commodities out of the warehouse and into the streets. When they arrived at the residence, Lawrence tried on two of the dominos and was asked to pay for the objects before Ward returned to the warehouse. Lawrence claimed he did not have enough cash in his possession to complete the transaction and subsequently left the house (dominos in hand) to find his friend for additional funds (whom one of the dominos was for). This action was mistaken as Lawrence attempting to steal the dominos, masks, and hat and feather rather than seeking more cash. The pursuit carried the dominos through Marylebone and Mayfair, around Chandos Street and New Cavendish Street. Ultimately Lawrence did not make it to the masquerade and was apprehended.

Throughout the pursuit the dominos operated as both commodity and costume. Until they were paid for, the dominos remained commodities from Ward's perspective, while Lawrence viewed them as necessary costumes as neither he nor his friend would be able to enter the ensuing masquerade without them. The

---

[67] *Old Bailey Proceedings Online* (www.oldbaileyonline.org, version 8.0, 15 September 2022), April 1796, trial of THOMAS LAWRENCE (t17960406-80).

demand for cash upfront upon delivery, despite mentions of credit, indicates a risk of letting out dominos, and pre-payment would ensure that in the event they were not returned the owner was not at a complete loss. Requiring payment and Ward's overzealous pursuit of Lawrence also point to the value of the domino as a reusable, loanable costume. These black silk dominos might go through repeated lettings, bringing Thomas profit multiple times over making the domino both a commodity and an investment. If stolen, Thomas not only lost the habits but also lost any potential future transactions that would accompany them. If Lawrence had planned to steal the dominos, he would have gained a masquerade habit that could either be pawned or turned into another garment – as Walpole mentioned in his correspondence. This shows the unique situation of the domino as a variable garment that held a range of meanings within the context of the warehouse and entertainment preparations, expanding beyond the popular reports of its dull nature inside the walls of the masquerade itself.

Warehouse and domino proximity to the masquerade venue became increasingly important as the entertainment grew in accessibility at the end of the century, making the quick-change nature of the domino more important than in previous years. While its flexibility and transmutability made it a popular choice in the 1770s and 1780s, the domino received more attention in advertisements and was tied to both chronological and geographical factors of convenience. A number of warehouses advertised the convenience of having a wide range of dominos on hand and being located next to, across from, or attached to masquerade venues, which would have limited the risk and exposure of the wealthy to the dangers of the streets of London. Lewis and Co. took care to draw attention to not only proximity to the Opera House, but also the extensive number of dominos available:

> They have taken the above Shop, only a few doors from the Opera House, where Ladies and Gentlemen may be accommodated with Apartments to dress, and Dresses to be had much to their advantage, having upwards of Two Hundred Dominos to let or sell on the lowest terms. The disagreeable inconvenience frequently found in obtaining a Coach, will here be obviated, the Warehouse being so contiguous to the Theatre, as to render that vehicle unnecessary after dressing.[68]

Warehouse owner J Green placed a similar advertisement, announcing his shop's closeness to King's Opera House, being 'only Two Doors from the Opera House. . . . Ladies and Gentlemen who please to honour him with their

---

[68] *Morning Post and Fashionable World*, 17 April 1795; further examples are found in the *Morning Chronicle*, the *World*, and the *Times* for warehouses of Bealby's, Wear's, Lewis and Co's, and Croft's.

commands, to observe, that his Warehouse is so contiguous to the Theatre, as to prevent the necessity of a Coach or a Person attending the Masks to the Theatre'.[69] In a later posting, Green reinforced this proximity and offered consumers a range of dominos they might choose from before walking to a masquerade at King's, 'Green respectfully acquaints the Nobility, Gentry, and the Public in general, that he has a large Assortment of Elegant Dominos, which he will be happy to accommodate them with, on the most reasonable terms . . . Good Dominos, as low as 7s. 6d. for hire'.[70] These advertisements not only indicate the altering business strategies of warehouse owners: they also imply a change in the temporal structure of the commercial masquerade and its belated shift to the wider leisure market. The ability to pick up a ready-made domino onsite, wear it over existing clothing, and return it immediately after the entertainment catered to a larger range of the population who may have been otherwise unable to acquire such items due to conflicting schedules with hours of employment. It also removed the additional expense of employing a carriage or chair for those who might not normally depend upon or afford such modes of transportation.

3.2 Language and Price

In masquerade warehouse ephemera, prices often followed descriptions and appeared on trade cards while choice adjectives were used on bills of sale to describe dominos. Looking at the vocabulary and prices provides a further layer of analysis and shows how cost or language could be indicative of quality when used jointly or alone. In his work on the consumer revolution, Neil McKendrick recognised the influence of newspaper advertisements in contributing to the increasing commercialisation of goods and experiences. He noted the complexity of crafting advertisements and their overlooked potential in contributing to economic and social history. McKendrick highlighted this in his exploration of the practices of a single advertiser, explaining the how tone, language, and audience could inform existing understandings of commercial practices.[71] Margaret Hunt similarly noted the growing significance of advertisements in eighteenth-century papers; however, her analysis of ephemeral commercial print moved beyond newspapers to include trade cards, bill heads, and tickets, among other items. These materials became increasingly widespread throughout the reading public, with advertisements and social news taking up more

---

[69] *Morning Post and Fashionable World*, 17 April 1795.   [70] *True Briton*, 23 January 1797.
[71] Neil McKendrick, 'George Packwood and the Commercialization of Shaving: The Art of Eighteenth-Century Advertising or "The Way to Get Money and Be Happy"', in *The Birth of a Consumer Society: the Commercialization of Eighteenth-Century England*, ed. John Brewer, Neil McKendrick, and J.H. Plumb (London: Europa, 1982), 147–9.

space in papers as the century progressed.[72] Both McKendrick and Hunt's work stresses that descriptive language in advertisements contributes important evidence relating to the experience of selling and consuming goods throughout the century. Cynthia Sundberg Wall reinforces this point in her study of descriptive language, arguing that as more goods became available, so too did the genres of description. Visual and textual sources circulated across social spaces, exposing contemporaries to a range of increasingly detailed depictions and building a 'common landscape of things'.[73] My analysis of the domino applies these approaches to show how it was a central component of the shared visual landscape of the masquerade. The following analysis also expands on these methodologies to examine how words and cost were linked to each other in this verbal marketplace. The domino's use as an advertising tool in these varied forms inspires a rethinking of the relationship between the domino and masquerade itself. The popularity of the domino, whether priced at seven shillings or three guineas, was concomitant with the growth of the masquerade and saw corresponding increases in availability, variety, and presence in masquerade spaces.

Examining the domino's steady presence in advertisements against fluctuations in description, price, and audience sheds new light on the domino's purpose, the intended consumer, and delayed commercialisation of the masquerade. Throughout the second half of the century the domino consistently appeared in masquerade warehouse advertisements and was regularly called out amidst the range of masquerade habits that warehouses had in stock. Its presence across warehouses, regardless of location or name, suggests that it was an integral part of the masquerade business and staple costume option for those wanting to attend a masquerade. Warehouses used descriptive language as a way to entice the reader, display their goods, and encourage continued business from their existing clientele. These advertisements illustrated an awareness of targeted consumers and followed the widely used 'puff boastful' style, claiming to sell dominos and masquerade habits that far surpassed the quality of others offered for sale. The 'puff superlative' was another form that also appeared widely across warehouse advertisements, referring to masquerade garments as being made from the best materials and available at the best prices.[74] Habit-maker Mr Clowes's advertisement included both styles,

---

[72] Margaret Hunt, *The Middling Sort: Commerce, Gender, and the Family in England 1680–1780* (Berkeley: University of California Press, 1996), 185; Jeremy Black, *The English Press in the Eighteenth Century* (Beckenham: Croom Helm, 1987), 26–7.

[73] Cynthia Sundberg Wall, *The Prose of Things: Transformations of Description in the Eighteenth Century* (London: University of Chicago Press, 2006), 165–6.

[74] McKendrick, 'George Packwood and the Commercialization of Shaving', 148–9.

employing superlatives to enhance his product inventory and a vague price point to appear affordable (bolded for emphasis):

> Mr. Clowes having met very great Encouragement from the Nobility and Gentry, &c. (his warehouse being more convenient than Tavistock-street) has induced him to lay in a **large variety of new dominos**, **elegantly trimmed**, in hopes of the continuance of their favours, which he will study to deserve, by a punctual, obedience and **reasonable charge**.[75]

Clowes identified his present and future clientele as the 'Nobility and Gentry' and alluded to his having served persons of high status in the past. These public associations with the upper ranks, while subject to the puff's exaggeratory nature, might encourage continued and new business from the elite and reinforces connections between the domino, masquerade, and persons of status. His mentions of having a 'large variety of new dominos' that are 'elegantly trimmed' illustrated consumer attraction to new rather than old or previously let dominos and Clowes' knowledge of their preference for embellished dominos. The decision to avoid a specific price point by listing his dominos at a 'reasonable' price encouraged interested parties to enquire and engage with the warehouse directly. This term remained vague until 1779, when Readshaw's warehouse tied 'reasonable' to letting a domino for 10s 6d, or half a guinea, for the night. These price points were baseline indicators with the full costs of domino rental often exceeding half a guinea by two to three times as much. This minimum price of 10s 6d was widely accepted and used across the masquerade warehouse industry, operating as a benchmark through the 1770s and 1780s. Like Clowes, Fletcher's warehouse and an unnamed warehouse at 401 Oxford Street echoed Clowes' descriptions. The unnamed warehouse promoted a 'great variety of superb Dominos, elegantly trimmed, to be Sold or Lett at 10s. 6d. for the Night' and Fletcher included details of trimming and colour, publicising his elegant dominos, also available to let at the 'reasonable rate' of 10s 6d for the evening.[76] The range in habit style and inclusion of elegant trimmings points to a demand for dominos that were convenient but not quotidian, while a minimum price point sets the tone for clientele expenditure. Providing a variety of options financially and materially allowed the client to customise their domino and display personal taste through colour and embellishment – much like the surviving pink and black dominos.

Warehouse owner A. Atkinson relied on language in newspaper advertisements, her warehouse name, and trade cards to feature the masquerade

---

[75] *London Evening Post*, 22–5 May 1773.

[76] Readshaw's in *Morning Post and Daily Advertiser*, 4 April 1779; 401 Oxford Street *Morning Herald and Daily Advertiser*, 3 March 1783; Fletcher's in *Morning Herald and Daily Advertiser*, 4 February 1784.

goods she sold, showing how the domino was a multifaceted marketing tool and, as Wall argues, contributed to a common landscape of masquerade things. In newspaper listings, Atkinson offered a 'great variety of new elegant Dominos ... ready for the Nobility and Gentry's inspection'. She put a particular emphasis on this in a later advertisement, reminding the elite that 'N.B. [they] may be accommodated with rich new dominos, both coloured and black, either trimmed or plain' at her warehouse.[77] The name of the warehouse left no questions about its purpose, with the straightforward title of 'The Domino and Mask Warehouse'. Atkinson's choice to use the domino as the warehouse's namesake indicates consumer knowledge of the habit's steadfast association with the masquerade and points to wider recognition of masquerade culture beyond the walls of the entertainment itself. The business's trade card reflected this, capturing the descriptive language of the newspapers and combining text with visual cues to signal the bond between the masquerade and domino (Figure 15). Images of three masks line the top of the trade card while 'Domino' and 'Mask' are written in a distinctive script across the middle – focusing the viewer's attention on the key products that she sells. The words 'elegant' and 'new' reappear, matching the language of her and her contemporaries' advertisements.[78] The absence of the word masquerade is also worthy of

Figure 15 William Darling, trade card of A. Atkinson, clothier, c.1775
© The Trustees of the British Museum. All rights reserved.

---

[77] *Morning Post and Daily Advertiser*, 11 April 1777; *Morning Post and Daily Advertiser*, 17 April 1780.

[78] Richman's Warehouse advertises dominos in both newspapers and on trade cards as well. The language is consistent across the two forms of print, describing the dominos as rich, new, elegant: 'Richman respectfully acquaints the Nobility and Gentry, that he has opened No. 361, two Doors from the Pantheon, Oxford-street, where he has a rich Variety and elegant Assortment of new Dominos to Let or Sell, on reasonable Terms'. *Public Advertiser*, 4 February 1784. Trade card in the Heal Collection at the British Museum.

note. Although Atkinson made it clear that she operated a masquerade warehouse in her newspaper listings, the omission of this label on her trade card indicated an unspoken, common understanding of masquerade culture, here expressed through the domino as a related verbal cue.

Clowes and Atkinson are two examples among many that employed descriptive words as the dominant component of their advertisements and regularly featured the domino as a main type of habit. Khlut's and Wayte's masquerade warehouses similarly addressed the elite and highlighted the quality of their dominos within their longer advertisements.[79] Khlut promised 'handsome' dominos from an 'elegant and extensive wardrobe', while Wayte boasted 'the greatest choice of new, elegant, and superb dominos' available to purchase or let and made at the shortest notice.[80] The repetitive use of elegant, new, and handsome described the expected quality and state of the domino, while descriptions of material characteristics provided visual hints of what one might wear or see at a masquerade. Silk was the most frequently mentioned fabric, though 'rich' was also used to describe the domino's materiality. In her extensive work on eighteenth-century silks, Natalie Rothstein explains that although it did not refer to a specific type of fabric, 'rich' was a frequent label for any type of high-quality material comparable to silk. She infers that this 'must have been quite clearly recognisable since the term occurs in invoices as well as in advertisements'.[81]

Warehouse owners Timewell and Moore included material details about quality, fabric, and colour in their advertisements throughout the 1770s and 1780s. Timewell specified having black and coloured silk dominos in addition to other fancy dresses and reprinted the respective text in subsequent years.[82] D. Moore included material and monetary details for his large stock of dominos and mentioned the domino enthusiastically throughout his lengthy advertisement: 'a great variety of new Dominos, particularly a number Dominos, particularly a number of rich black silk ditto . . . Likewise a great variety of fancy dresses, and Dominos'.[83] He specified two rental rates for these dominos: the rich black silk option at one guinea for the evening with the other non-descriptive domino at half a guinea. This price variation and the use of 'rich' demarcates an implicit noticeable difference in quality between the two styles of

---

[79] A few other notable masquerade warehouses that consistently listed dominos in their advertisements include Timewell's, Pritchard's, Brackstone's, Griffitt's, Sowden's, and Jackson's.

[80] *Morning Post and Daily Advertiser*, 16 January 1777; *Morning Post and Daily Advertiser*, 31 March 1780.

[81] Rothstein, *Silk Designs of the Eighteenth Century*, 294.

[82] *Public Ledger*, 3 May 1774, again in the *Gazetteer and New Daily Advertiser*, 27 April 1775 and 2 December 1776; *Oracle and Public Advertiser*, 2 February 1797.

[83] *Morning Herald and Daily Advertiser*, 3 March 1783.

domino and the expectations of domino quality associated with these varying price points. A revised version circulated the following year, listing the same domino options again, but positioned the cheaper domino option first, as 10s 6d, and the rich silk dominos second, at £1 1s. Shifting the language from the guinea to sterling and changing the order of the products suggests that a change in consumer audience may have begun, as indicated simultaneously by a slow move to lowered masquerade ticket prices that same year. The decision to reprint their advertisements across the span of a few years, or in some cases, decades, showed consistency in linguistic style and the warehouses' dependency on the domino as a profitable masquerade staple and persistent choice of masquerade dress.

Masquerade warehouse advertisements began more widely shifting and integrating new words and approaches around 1785, which maps directly onto the commercial changes that the masquerade was experiencing through the late 1780s and 1790s. During the final decade of the century, masquerade proprietors finally began lowering ticket prices from two guineas to a half guinea or one guinea each. Although this dropped ticket costs into a price range that was more accessible to the middling sorts, a new option to purchase separate supper spaces and the continued practice of occupying theatre boxes allowed the upper ranks to maintain their distance and mingle with their peers rather than the general public. This change is reflected in the language used to describe the domino in masquerade warehouse advertisements. While still seeking to appeal to the elite, there is a clear shift in tone to include the middling sort in the domino market. Many warehouse owners continued to address the nobility and gentry, but expanded this to include 'the Public' or replaced their audience with 'Ladies and Gentlemen'. Richman's warehouse revised their earlier advertisements, addressing the 'Nobility, Gentry, and Public in general', while J. Green consistently targeted 'Ladies and Gentlemen who please to honour him with their command'.[84] The language around the domino also became more variable, expanding the range of quality beyond just the very best and most elegant to dominos 'of an inferior kind'.[85] There is not much listed beyond this – Moore advertised 'a few inferior Silk Dominos' available to let at five shillings, but did not expand on what 'inferior' means.[86] The price alone points to a shabby barebones domino without any trimmings or embellishments. Thinking along the lines of Rothstein, 'inferior' might have been used similarly to 'rich' to refer broadly to the quality of a garment and was understood to visually and

---

[84] *Morning Herald*, 30 May 1792; *Morning Post and Fashionable World*, 17 April 1795.

[85] *Morning Chronicle and London Advertiser*, 6 February 1787 for Warden's Warehouse; *World*, 4 May 1789.

[86] *Gazetteer and New Daily Advertiser*, 26 April 1790.

physically reflect this when worn. The use of 'inferior' in warehouse advertisements solely referred to dominos rather than also applying to other forms of masquerade habit, suggesting that the domino was the most affordable option to those who might now be able to attend the masquerade as ticket prices began to drop.

As warehouse owners became more upfront about offering inferior or cheaper domino options, they also publicised the upper end of their price range, showing they were still capable of making and supplying the elite with habits suitable to their fashionable tastes. Donnelly's circulated a range of advertisements exhibiting this. Some listings focused on dominos available for purchase at the hefty price of £4 4s, while others included details of dominos to let on 'the most reasonable terms'.[87] Subsequent postings provided details of both within the same line: 'New Dominos for sale, made elegant and full, at 4 l. 4s. Those for hire from 7s 6d. To 1 l. 1s.'[88] Fawcett's warehouse also printed advertisements reflecting a growing consumer base. The first highlighted 'New and elegant black and coloured Dominos and Masks to be Sold, for three pounds thirteen shillings and six-pence each', while another listed the warehouse as a place for cheap masquerade dresses with elegant dominos available to let.[89] The high price point of dominos available to purchase at both Donnelly's and Fawcett's indicates continued elite participation and patronage while the addition of 'cheap' and lowered price of 7s 6d for let dominos reflects increasing demand of the middling ranks. Focusing on the domino in this way and using a spectrum of adjectives to describe it as a rich or inferior quality also shows the warehouse owners' recognition of a widening market for the domino and their desire to encourage sales outside of the upper ranks of society.

3.3 The Inventory of James Spilsbury

Newspaper advertisements were not the only place where descriptive language was used in relation to the domino. The auction list of James Spilsbury's masquerade warehouse inventory is a comprehensive source that employed a similar set of words to describe the various lots available for purchase. This list substantiates the importance of the domino in advertisements and the material evidence provided by dominos in existing collections. The crossover

---

[87] *Morning Post and Daily Advertiser*, 14 February 1789; *Argus*, 5 February 1790; *Morning Chronicle*, 22 May 1793.

[88] *Public Advertiser or Political and Literary Diary*, 20 February 1794.

[89] *Morning Post and Fashionable World*, 2 June 1795; *Oracle and Public Advertiser*, 23 February 1797; references to cheaper dominos in: *Morning Herald*, 21 January 1797. Goodacre's Warehouse also stressed domino availability at the same price point: 'N.B. New Dominos, full trimmed, and all complete, at 3l. 13s. 6d. each'; *Morning Herald*, 27 April 1792.

of words like rich, silk, 'trimm'd', and identification of colour shows that while the purpose of an advertisement was to encourage consumer business, their descriptions did not stray far from the practical vocabulary of the masquerade or contemporary garments. Using quantitative and qualitative approaches to analyse the domino within Spilsbury's inventory highlights the significance of the domino within the warehouse industry, reinforcing its place as an integral source of income and a staple needed to meet the demand of masquerade goers. The inventory data also supplies additional context for the extant physical dominos and supplements the evidence their materiality provides. Together, this evidence shows how the domino was a dependable masquerade habit for sellers and consumers, offering convenience, flexibility, and customisability that allowed warehouse owners to cater to clients and clients to display their status through material taste.

Spilsbury's auction inventory came from his and his wife's long history in the masquerade and warehouse industry. James and Judith Spilsbury (née Pritchard) both came from millinery backgrounds and had begun their involvement in the masquerade habit industry during the late 1760s. Their masquerade warehouse grew with the help of family connections and their shared knowledge of the trade. It also benefitted from the continued support of elite clientele, including the Duchess of Bedford, the Earl of Winterton, the Duchess of Ancaster, and the wife of the Lord Chancellor, Agneta Yorke. The Spilsburys' warehouse was in operation until 1779, when a public auction at Christie's marked James' retirement.[90] The decision to auction the remaining inventory rather than leave it to his replacement suggests James saw potential for profitability based on previous knowledge about the demand within the industry and his customer base. The details of this auction can be found in the existing catalogue at Christie's, which has until now, been overlooked as a significant source in understanding the masquerade and its related costumes – the domino in particular. Looking at the prevalence of dominos in Spilsbury's inventory and the language used to describe them sheds light on the actuality of the warehouse rather than the image put out to the public in papers. Out of the 290 masquerade habits listed, 104 (36%) were dominos. Considering over one third of Spilsbury's stock was made up of this singular type of habit marks the domino as a significant part of the masquerade business. A quick glance at the list of auction buyers reinforces this, revealing that competitors Timewell and Thomas attended and purchased a selection of habits from Spilsbury – most of which

---

[90] *Public Advertiser*, 27 January 1779; *Gazetteer and New Daily Advertiser*, 29 January 1779; *A Catalogue of the genuine, rich and very expensive Wardrobe Consisting of a Great Variety of Masquerade Dresses, the Property of Mr. Spilsbury*, auction by Mess. Christie and Ansell (Christie and Ansell's: London), 4 and 5 February 1779.

were dominos.[91] This makes Spilsbury's list nominally representative of his contemporaries, who saw the auction as an opportunity to expand their own wardrobes and increase their supply of the popular and timeless domino. The high presence of dominos in Spilsbury's stock and interest of his peers indicates a relatively high demand for this type of habit during the years he and his fellow warehouse people were in business.[92] If we take the numbers from Spilsbury and the consistent presence of the domino in contemporary masquerade warehouse advertisements as jointly representative of the industry at large, it becomes apparent that the domino was a central fixture within masquerade transactions and the masquerade itself.

Breaking the dominos into further descriptive categories based on the language used in the auction list provides a clearer picture of what was available and worn at masquerades during the second half of the century (Table 1). Spilsbury's list reinforces the significant characteristics of the domino that were valued by masquerade warehouse owners and consumers alike. These align with the descriptions in newspaper advertisements and include descriptions of colour, quality, and embellishment. The colour or colours of the domino appear alongside each lot for auction, indicating the importance of colour as a point of interest and distinction. A detailed breakdown of colour can be seen in Table 1, which shows that, like the extant dominos from Section 2, this habit came in a wide spectrum beyond the classic Venetian black. The most popular colours here rank as black, pink, and white, which maps directly onto the dominos earlier discussed and suggests they are fairly representative of the domino's place within wider masquerade culture. Horace Walpole's preference for a purple domino and James Brudenell's selection of a straw and purple one mark the popularity of both single and multicoloured dominos.[93] Spilsbury's stock underpins this trend as it contains more non-black options than it does the classic black. Of the 104 dominos listed, 71 are not black (68%) and 62 use more than one colour, like Brudenell's and Frances Burney's Miss Strange.[94] While the auction catalogue shows it was relatively normal for non-black dominos to use a range of colours, including black, as trim or lining, this was not the case for purely black dominos, which remained a singular shade.[95] The presence of

---

[91] Thomas purchased twenty-two of Spilsbury's lots, thirteen of which were dominos. Timewell also purchased thirteen dominos of his total thirty-four lots, which was proportionally smaller than Thomas's but makes up one third of his total acquisition.

[92] Carole Shammas, 'Changes in English and Anglo-American Consumption from 1550 to 1800', in *Consumption and the World of Goods*, ed. John Brewer and Roy Porter (London: Routledge, 1993).

[93] See Section 2.2, 'Materiality'.

[94] *A Catalogue of the genuine, rich and very expensive Wardrobe Consisting of ... Mr. Spilsbury.*

[95] Select examples include: 'a white domino trim'd with lilach, a green [domino] with red and black, a most elegant pink colour domino spangled all over with silver, white and blue trimming'.

Table 1 Descriptive language in Spilsbury's auction inventory

Category	Inventory sub-category	Total
Garment body colour	Black	29
	Blue	5
	Buff	1
	Crimson	1
	Green	12
	Grey	5
	Lilac	6
	Orange	1
	Pink/Rose	15
	Pompadour	2
	White	22
	Yellow	1
	Unknown	4
Colouring	Single colour	38
	Multicolour	62
	Non-black	71
Descriptive word	Trim'd/Trimm'd	62
	Flowers	3
	Pink'd	3
	Rich	22

colour found in this list and in the existing physical dominos as well as in earlier personal masquerade experiences challenges the overwhelming reports of black dominos dominating masquerade spaces throughout the period, indicating that masquerades were perhaps more vibrant than expected.

The descriptive language of contemporary advertisements also appeared in the auction list, describing domino quality and embellishments. The frequent use of 'trimm'd' and 'rich' mirrored this vocabulary and contributed to a textual and aural picture of the dominos as auction attendees read the catalogue and the auctioneer called each lot aloud. Applying these words to some but not all of the dominos shows discretion and an understanding of difference between domino styles and material quality. Emphasising these two characteristics in particular also points to an awareness of consumer expectations and demands – the option to express taste through embellishment and status through richness provided various ways for the upper ranks to reveal parts of their identity despite being in disguise. This is especially visible through the recurring use of contrasting trim, which would have incurred additional expense. Over half of Spilsbury's dominos were described as being trimmed, allowing the wearer to display their taste and rank while unique colour combinations would make their identity less challenging to discover. The pink and black dominos in existing collections highlight how trim and embellishments could enhance the basic domino from a simple habit to fashionable one that reflected elite status.

As Spilsbury's bulk of dominos and its consistent presence in advertisements show, the domino was the most popular and accessible masquerade habit. While this may have been in part due to its ease of wear and the ability to customise it as desired, the domino's varying price points, ranging from five shillings to six pounds or more, made it equally attractive as a convenient and affordable option. The dominos in Spilsbury's auction sit nicely within this range, with 8s 6d as the lowest price and £2 19s the highest. These prices represent a transactional agreement between the seller and buyer and an understanding of what each domino's quality should be, based on the descriptive language used. The buyer would not pay beyond what they thought acceptable for a plain, rich, or trimmed domino and Spilsbury or the auctioneer would not accept anything below the starting offer. When looking at price in relation to language, it becomes clear that the dominos with additional descriptive language to colour were of a higher quality than those without. Rothstein's interpretation of 'rich' becomes evident with only one rich domino being sold at £1 and the remaining averaging £1 15s between them. The prices of dominos with trim were similarly higher than the frequently advertised reasonable rate of seven shillings, averaging £1 4s and taking them out of the 'affordable' category and into the price point of the upper ranks. Both Timewell and Thomas purchased dominos for their own inventories at these rates, signalling that these were either going as a bargain or reasonable price and the prices were therefore indicative of averages one might encounter when looking for a domino prior to a masquerade. Timewell and Thomas's buys and these averages demonstrate that most dominos within a warehouse's wardrobe sat above the price point listed in newspapers and, not unlike bargain sections in stores today, the warehouses used the lower end of the price spectrum as ways to draw interested masqueraders into the shop before upselling them with their larger quantity of more expensive options.

Bills of sale and personal accounts further reveal that standard prices of let and purchased dominos sat above a guinea from the 1760s up through the early 1800s. Although the auction list predates the masquerade's shift to wider commercialisation that began around 1785, these sources show that the actual selling and letting price of the domino did not necessarily reflect the changes seen in language in advertising. Brudenell begrudgingly paid two guineas to hire a domino in 1763, which was at least 'better than giving 4 Guineas & ½ to have it entirely to myself'.[96] The bill of sale issued to the Earl of Winterton in 1772 also listed the cost of hiring a domino, with his payment to Spilsbury totalling £3 3s and far exceeding the then baseline price of 10s 6d. The 1796 trial of Thomas Lawrence over the theft of two black silk dominos, hats, and masks likewise valued the dominos jointly at 30s, leaving them 15s each. The accusing party was none other than Thomas, the same warehouse owner who attended Spilsbury's auction and purchased a selection of dominos and other various dresses. Thomas's consistent appearance across these sources shows that even seventeen years later there was not a significant drop in domino values.[97] Two additional bills of sale from the early 1800s include details of similar pricing that ranged above the frequently listed five shillings. The first, issued to the Prince of Wales, showed a purchase of '1 Black Domino, Mask, & Bahute' sold for £1 11s 6p.[98] The distinction between the mask and 'bahute' hints that the bahute here referred to the Venetian *mantellina*, which would have been worn as a partner piece to the mask. This distinction may also point to the Prince of Wales purchasing two styles of mask – the first 'mask' being the generic eye mask with draping fabric (Figure 2) and the second referring to the white Venetian *bauta* (Figure 1). While this purchase contained more than just the domino, these extra components were accessory and would not have impacted the total cost beyond a few shillings.[99] The second bill of sale from Brooks and Heath likewise listed the cost of a domino at one guinea.[100] Although these bills of sale are predominately representative of purchases made among the upper sorts, the other sources used throughout this section have highlighted that the prices listed in these bills are not unique to these individuals, but rather reflective of wider trends in price. The case at the Old Bailey and Spilsbury's auction inventory make this particularly clear and show that even 'reasonable' or cheap habits were still unaffordable for the majority of Georgian society, contributing to the overall financial inaccessibility of the masquerade and its role as a socially exclusive entertainment.

4 Everywhere and Nowhere

Regular reports of the masquerade spread textual depictions of the entertainment through newspapers and in columns entitled 'Masquerade Intelligence'.

---

[96] James Brudenell, MSS 9/35/316.

[97] *Old Bailey Proceedings Online*. Trial of Thomas Lawrence.

[98] Bill of Sale from H. Wayte, 8 February 1802, MSS GEO/MAIN/29315, Royal Archives.

[99] Masks were normally between two and five shillings.

[100] *Household Bills and Vouchers of Thomas Whitmore*, June 6, 1807, Whitmore Family of Orsett Estate, D/DWt/A1, Essex Record Office.

These accounts helped to recreate the evening's entertainment for the reader as they included descriptions of the venue and provided critical commentary on the costumes and persons who were present. More often than not, the authors noted that most masquerades were filled with overwhelming numbers of dull, black dominos. These descriptions contrasted contemporary depictions of broad masquerade scenes, which seldom portrayed dominos, focusing instead on a variety of character disguises in their masquerade scenes. This section will examine these conflicting representations of the domino and what they reveal about real experiences and imagined perceptions of the masquerade as well as how these varying presentations of the masquerade inform past and present understandings of the masquerade's place within eighteenth-century social history and leisure culture.

This analysis engages with a similar methodology to Melanie Doderer-Winkler and her work on eighteenth-century illuminations and temporary entertainment structures, which has highlighted the importance of using visual, textual, and material sources to establish new narratives in history. The scholarship of Vickery, Anishanslin, and Van Horn is equally significant in shaping this analysis and the way it incorporates evidence gathered from a wide range of sources.[101] Employing evidence from newspapers, printed ephemera, and manuscripts sheds light on how the domino functioned in reality and how its use and reputation impacted wider engagement with it in masquerade settings. These sources include reports taken from a cohort study of over 2,500 newspapers in the Burney Collection, surviving masquerade tickets in the collections of the British Museum and Museum of London, and manuscript accounts of several masquerade participants. Scenes from contemporary literature (*Amelia* and *Cecilia*) likewise contribute useful evidence about shared cultural knowledge of the domino and its ubiquitous presence in masquerade spaces. The relative absence of the domino across visual depictions of masquerades, seen in prints and engravings as well as on handkerchiefs, supplies crucial insight into how the entertainment was imagined and could be edited to communicate an appealing idealisation of the masquerade that would benefit the commercial side of the entertainment. This is seen in prints and engravings from the British Museum, Lewis Walpole Library, and the author's own collections and two existing handkerchiefs in the Victoria and Albert Museum and Museum of London. These representations of the masquerade provide a different reality

[101] Melanie Doderer-Winkler, *Magnificent Entertainments: Temporary Architecture for Georgian Festivals* (London: Yale University Press, 2013); Van Horn, *The Power of Objects in Eighteenth-Century British America*; Anishanslin, *Portrait of a Woman in Silk*; Amanda Vickery, *Behind Closed Doors: At Home in Georgian England* (London: Yale University Press, 2009).

of the masquerade, suggesting that the domino was absent from the entertainment, and contribute to the creation of an idealised version of the entertainment – one that aligned with anticipatory expectations and cultural tropes rather than reality.

4.1 The Domino Everywhere

As Section 3 has illustrated, the domino was a significant part of the masquerade warehouse industry and appeared seemingly everywhere in advertisements throughout the 1770s, 1780s, and 1790s. Newspaper reports of masquerade scenes, predominantly printed in the column 'Masquerade Intelligence', simultaneously indicated that the presence of the domino overflowed from warehouses and into the entertainment itself. These accounts circulated in the days following masquerades and increasingly included disparaging commentary about the overuse of the domino among participants. The black domino received particular criticism with papers calling masqueraders lazy, selfish, and boring. In one of many accounts, the *Middlesex Journal or Chronicle of Liberty* recounted 'the dominos were about three to one in proportion to all the rest [of the masquerade habits]' at a Pantheon masquerade in 1773.[102] A decade later, newspapers were still including the overwhelming presence of dominos in their pages, though not always impassively. The masquerade writer for *The Morning Post* complained that while 'above nine hundred persons assembled last night at the Opera House … Dominos *predominated* as usual.'[103] Just as masquerades became a regular fixture within the social calendar, so did dominos become a consistent and notably dull aspect of the masquerade scene.

With elite attendance fuelling these masked entertainments, it is not surprising that participants became jaded and costume creation transitioned from exciting to tedious. Concocting clever disguises and performing different characters each week was demanding and time-consuming. In one instance, a domino-clad masquerade attendee explained that due to his last-minute decision to attend, he and his companions did not have enough time 'to make up such dresses as they would wish to show themselves in'.[104] They chose the domino instead; it offered a practical alternative for those who decided to attend masquerades at the last minute or were weary of the demands of character and

---

[102] *The Middlesex Journal or Chronicle of Liberty*, 13–15 May 1773; *Morning Chronicle and London Advertiser*, 16 February 1774; *St. James's Chronicle or the British Evening Post*, 19–21 December 1775; *Morning Chronicle and London Advertiser*, 4 December 1776; *General Evening Post*, 29–31 January 1778; *London Courant and Westminster Chronicle*, 3 May 1780; these are a few additional examples, but there are many more similar reports that circulated from 1768 through the end of the century.

[103] *Morning Post*, 1 May 1784.   [104] *General Evening Post*, 1–3 March 1770.

fancy dress (or simply wanted to spectate from the shadows). The domino was 'vastly convenient to throw over every thing' and offered innumerable options for customisation that would display rank and taste without demanding much of the wearer.[105] The extant dominos in the first section exhibit these appealing characteristics, and the relationship between the domino and masquerade warehouse further solidifies its place within the entertainment and wardrobes of the upper ranks.

Public opinion viewed the domino differently and labelled it as a lazy, lacklustre, and overall uninspiring choice of dress. The black domino in particular was the target of much censure throughout newspapers, who criticised its overwhelming presence and overuse by men of rank.[106] The *Gazetteer and New Daily Advertiser* put the onus on the elite, observing 'the number of Dominos seemed greater than usual – an evident sign that the people of fashion are beginning to grow tired, and that they are willing to screen their indolence under this insipid mask'.[107] Numerous papers echoed this sentiment, associating the constant presence of the domino with the elite and complaining of its dull and wearisome nature. The *Morning Post* recalled 'A great many persons of distinction were present in dominos . . . Dukes of Cumberland, Manchester, and Ancaster', while the *Morning Post* and *Morning Chronicle* both cited various people of fashion in the habit.[108] The steady reports of this dull, domino-shrouded surplus indicated that it remained a favoured masquerade habit despite growing critiques of their 'boring' nature.

Though colourful dominos populated masquerade spaces alongside their black counterparts, the black domino remained a consistent choice of dress among the elite men. This may have been in part due to their experiences on the Grand Tour, which would have introduced them to the black Venetian domino and its use among the upper ranks. Adopting the black domino within the British masquerade scene is however, somewhat hypocritical, as the overuse of the black domino was criticised in personal accounts of *carnavale*.[109] The Prince of Wales, future George IV, was regularly spotted wearing a black domino, which is also supported in a related bill of sale from H. Wayte. The *Morning Post and Daily Advertiser* went as far as labelling this group as the 'black domino gentry'

---

[105] *Morning Chronicle and London Advertiser*, 7 March 1777.

[106] *Morning Post and Daily Advertiser*, 18 July 1776; *London Chronicle*, 1–3 February 1781; *Morning Herald and Daily Advertiser*, 11 June 1781; *General Advertiser and Morning Intelligencer*, 26 January 1782; *St James's Chronicle*, 19–21 April 1787; *World*, 2 February 1788; *Morning Herald*, 6 February 1788; *London Chronicle*, 28–31 March 1789; *Public Advertiser*, 21 May 1790.

[107] *Gazetteer and New Daily Advertiser*, 29 May 1772.

[108] *Morning Post*, 8 May 1776; *Independent Chronicle*, 18–21 May 1770; *Morning Chronicle*, 12 February 1772; *Middlesex Journal and Evening Advertiser*, 28 February–2 March 1775.

[109] Eglin, *Venice Transfigured*, 56.

and criticised their inability to dress creatively and contribute to the entertainment of a masquerade evening.[110] Lord Peterborough was also identified on multiple occasions sporting this habit, which was most likely the 'rich black domino' Lady Peterborough purchased for him at the Spilsbury warehouse auction in 1779.[111] The black domino transcended the boundaries of the city, appearing at masquerades in country residences of the elite as well. After attending a masquerade at Wargrave, the seat of Lord Barrymore, Lybbe Powys recalled there were 'Numbers of fancy dresses and many good masques, and a great many black dominoes; my lord [Barrymore] and all his party in these, and unmasked … Mr. Powys, myself, and our two sons [also] in black dominoes'.[112] It seemed that the domino was spreading through the elite space but did not often receive censure from the elites themselves.

The accounts of the Duchess of Northumberland and Horace Walpole similarly pointed to the domino's widespread use among the gentry and nobility but from a neutral rather than critical voice – each gave equal attention to the domino, fancy dress, and character dress in their descriptive masquerade scenes. Lady Elizabeth Percy consistently listed the names of masquerade participants and details of their costumes indiscriminately in her diary entries, citing over half the guests at a given masquerade wearing the publicly censored domino. She included details of embellishment, colour, and jewels, much in the same manner she described the elaborate fancy dress of others present. Despite wider opinions of the domino being dull, she does not seem bothered by the domino's presence, but rather more so by its appearance, materiality, and cleanliness. She herself borrows a domino for a masquerade, paying over £4 in the 1740s. Horace Walpole did not seem adversely affected by the domino either, reporting others wearing them and suggesting it as a possible costume to a friend – using his own experience as a point of reference.[113] Another unidentified masquerade participant described a scene at King's Theatre, noting that 'The crowd was very great and twas much too full to distinguish half the fine dresses. A great many were in Dominos of both Sexes, but especialy men'.[114] She continued on to include descriptions of the elaborate and spectacular costumes she witnessed as well as the dominos worn by the King of Denmark and other members of the nobility. The author's attention to the various costumes (character, fancy dress,

---

[110] Royal Archives, GEO/MAIN/29315; *Morning Post and Daily Advertiser*, 9 February 1785.

[111] *London Chronicle*, 1–3 February 1781; *Morning Herald and Daily Advertiser*, 23 April 1782; *A Catalogue of the genuine, rich and very expensive Wardrobe Consisting of … Mr. Spilsbury*.

[112] Emily J. Climenson, ed., *Passages from the Diaries of Mrs. Phillip Lybbe Powys* (London: Longmans, Green, and Co., 1899), 249.

[113] Walpole, 'Letter to Horace Mann', 28 May 1763.

[114] Unknown author and addressee, 'Details of fancied dress etc … ', c.1780, MSS L30/14/435/12, The Wrest Park Papers, Bedfordshire Archives.

and domino) and relative indifference to the presence of each give further insight into attitudes among masquerade participants who were not bothered by the domino but rather saw it as a regular part of the evening's entertainment. Her observation of the domino's popularity among the crowd is equally significant as it aligned with the disparaging newspaper reports that focused on the men of the gentry and nobility as the main culprits of abusing the convenience and characterlessness of the domino.

The continued use of the black or other colour domino suggests that the masquerade was not about transgression and identity bending, but rather a space of sociability that required frequent attendance and might result in the elite, whose regular attendance was expected, resorting to a more steadfast and reusable form of costume that would still allow for visual display of status through dress. Those attending the masquerade in the domino cloak and mask seemed indifferent to the presence of others dressed similarly, presenting a different perspective than the criticisms that circulated in the papers. These varying ideas about the domino suggest that there was a disjunction between the idealised cultural expectations of a masquerade and its reality. Contemporary literature supplies helpful additional insight here, offering a balance between critical and nonchalant attitudes towards the ubiquitous domino. The fictional masquerade scenes of *Amelia* and *Cecilia* speak to the domino's role as a consistent feature of the masquerade experience while also highlighting a wider recognition and awareness of what a domino was physically and its multi-purpose functionality.

Though published in 1752 and thus before the height of masquerade culture began, Henry Fielding's *Amelia* is an early example of how the domino was becoming a central component of masquerade and literary language. Throughout the pivotal masquerade scene, though filled with descriptions of character masquerade dress and the venue itself, Fielding neglects to elaborate on the appearance of several types of dominos beyond their colour – if even that. He references the domino of the later revealed Mrs James as a 'blue domino', refers to Lord Ellison as a 'He Domino', and does not supply any additional details beyond Mr Booth, Colonel James, or Amelia's/Mrs Atkinson's dress other than their being dominos.[115] The absence of additional language to establish the characteristics of the domino highlights it was a common and expected part of a masquerade – real or imagined – much like a description of the diamond-patterned suit was normally absent from mentions of a person dressed in Harlequin costume.

---

[115] Henry Fielding, *Amelia*, Book X, Chapter 2, in *The Wesleyan Edition of the Works of Henry Fielding*, ed. Martin C. Battestin (Oxford: Oxford University Press, 1984), 412.

Fielding's decision to dress each of the main characters in the domino, which include Amelia (who is later discovered as Mrs Atkinson), Mr Booth, Colonel James, Mrs James, and Lord Ellison, points its potential use among the middling and upper ranks. Acting as a common disguise across these characters despite their gender and class differences sheds further light on two main aspects of the domino's key points of attraction and growing presence everywhere: convenience and transferability. Amelia relies on the domino's transferability to foil her husband's attempt to bring her to a masquerade at Ranelagh Gardens. She engages Mrs Atkinson in a change of places just as the party set off toward the entertainment, running back into the house to grab her mask where she 'whipt off her Domino, and threw it over Mrs. *Atkinson*, who stood ready to receive it, and ran immediately down Stairs, and stepping into *Amelia's* Chair proceeded with the rest to the Masquerade'.[116] Mrs James employs a domino switch as well, though hers is one of colours rather than bodies. Swapping black for blue enables her to separate herself from her husband at the masquerade and converse freely with Mr Booth about him. She reveals this later, sharing 'it is not so unusual a Thing, I believe, you yourself know to change Dresses,–I own I did it' and pointing to the convenience of the domino as quick disguise that was easily transportable and changeable.[117] As women of middling and upper-middling rank, the domino would have been a financially accessible option for Amelia/Mrs Atkinson and Mrs James, as well as their husbands. Unlike their wives, Mr Booth's and Colonel James' dressing in the black domino was less exceptional, and though it aligned with their financial status, it also cast them in a negative light as masqueraders who were willing to attend but not actively participate in the entertainment. Lord Ellison's use of the habit at this and previous masquerades likewise illustrates this attitude and reflects the domino's growing attraction, showing signs of it being 'everywhere', particularly among men. Dressing each of these five characters in dominos points to the habit's earlier association with and prevalence in masquerade spaces without the negative connotations of later decades. This highlights the domino's long-standing associations with the masquerade in both real and imagined scenes and suggests that changes in attitude to its presence shifted as it replaced character dress and became a common choice of the elite.

Cecilia, published in 1782 during the peak of masquerades, echoes this language and reflects wider cultural knowledge about the growing overuse of the domino in masquerade spaces. Burney's description of the masquerade viewing party at the Harrels' is not unlike those in newspapers and shows an awareness of this habit being 'everywhere', noting, 'Dominos of no character,

---

[116] Fielding, Book X, Chapter 3, 422.   [117] Fielding, Book XI, Chapter 1, 453.

and fancy-dresses of no meaning, made, as is usual at such meetings, the general herd of the company'.[118] Burney further draws upon the readers' assumed knowledge of the domino and its cultural and social assignations, introducing Mortimer Delvile, Cecilia's eventual love interest and future husband, as 'a white domino, who for a few minutes had been a very attentive spectator' – a title he retains throughout the scene and subsequent chapters until his identity is discovered.[119] The lack of descriptive language here indicates the readers' familiarity with this habit and ability to imagine it as part of the visual landscape of the masquerade. Burney's choice to employ a domino as Delvile's disguise and subsequently use it as his main identifying feature, in addition to his gentleman-like behaviour, reiterates several important points about the domino in Georgian culture concerning who wore it and why it was a popular choice of dress. Mortimer Delvile's character, though unknown by name at the time of his introduction, is dependent on the white domino to represent his nature to both the reader and Cecilia. As the only son of an upper-middling family, Mortimer carries the reputation and pride of his family with him, thus making the domino an appropriate choice of disguise. This would have aligned with existing knowledge about the domino habit and its use among men who were aspiring middling, gentry, and nobility. The neutral state of this dress would allow Mortimer to participate in the masquerade viewing party with as much or as little interaction as he desired. As the scene unravels, his continued efforts to dissuade an irksome devil from harassing Cecilia make his attentiveness and sensibility plain, neatly fitting him into the role of 'gentleman in a domino'. While newspapers were quick to censure this 'type' of masquerader, their criticisms centred on those who continually wore black dominos; colourful options like white, pink, or green, though still dull, were more kindly received. Mortimer's wearing a white domino therefore signals his taste, not unlike the portrait of Francis Osborne (Figure 8), and singles him out visually and linguistically from the potential overabundance of black dominos he might expect to encounter in masquerade spaces.

The use of the dominos across characters of differing ranks in the above texts and as advertising tools for masquerade warehouses indicate that the wealthy elite was not the only group who chose the domino as a main disguise at masquerades. The middling professions who aspired to attend a masquerade, even if only once, found the costume as a way to gain entry to this expensive entertainment. Though easily affordable among the elite, the price of the domino – hired or purchased – would have remained a notable expense for

---

[118] Frances Burney, *Cecilia, or Memoirs of an Heiress*, Vol. 1, Book II, ed. Peter Sabor and Margaret Anne Doody (London: 1782), 107.

[119] Burney, Vol. 1, Book II.

the upper-middling sorts – ranging from five shillings to half a guinea. This plus the cost of a ticket would place the total expense of masquerade attendance between one and a half and three guineas, making repeated middling participation an infrequent but attainable reality.[120] One newspaper identified a group of 'petty clerks in the city' who had the 'fashionable assurance to appear dressed in dominos', judging that this behaviour was too extravagant and foolish for men in such positions.[121] When complaining about the overabundance of black dominos at Carlisle House, the *Morning Chronicle* revealed 'Bankers, Clerks, Lottery Office Keepers, Players, and Newspaper Editors' among those using the thoughtless habit to join the masquerade and thus contributed to the overall dullness of the evening. That same evening, a group of butchers thought they might be able to pass as gentlemen under the guises of the classic black domino; however, their unruly behaviour was more telling than their habits were concealing, indicating that decorum was as much a part of the masquerade as disguise.[122]

Middling use of the domino may have helped increase this social group's attendance at masquerades; however, it did not increase their chances of mingling and conversing with their social superiors. As Hannah Greig has shown in her work on pleasure gardens, merely sharing an experience or social space did not guarantee sociability across ranks.[123] Even if the domino functioned as the disguise of the middling professions, the gentry and nobility remained comparably out of reach due to the use of partitioned space and their own disinterest in their social inferiors. These obstacles, as well as wider calls to action against the black domino from impresarios and masquerade hosts, worked against the 'equalising' nature of the habit and helped the elite retain their exclusive space despite widening commercialisation of leisure and the masquerade in the 1790s and 1800s.

4.2 Domino Bans

As the previous section makes clear, the versatility of the domino meant it was everywhere. Elites wore the domino due to its convenience and potential for conspicuous display, while middling professions might use it to gain once-in-a-lifetime entry to what they hoped to a be a night of revelry and intrigue. Reports of too many middling dominos or an overwhelming presence of black dominos could tarnish a venue's reputation of fashionability or brilliance and

---

[120] Table 4 in Kobza, 'Dazzling or Fantastically Dull', 171.
[121] *Middlesex Journal and Evening Advertiser*, 22–4 February 1774.
[122] *Morning Chronicle and London Advertiser*, 4 December 1776.
[123] Hannah Greig, '"All Together and All Distinct": Public Sociability and Social Exclusivity in London's Pleasure Gardens, ca. 1740–1800', *Journal of British Studies* 51 (2012): 50–75.

cost them the patronage of the upper ranks. Recognising this problematic nature of the domino, some impresarios and hosts worked to restrict its presence within their entertainments and instituted domino bans. Attempts to implement domino bans at commercial venues, like Carlisle House and the Pantheon, reveal that while the domino was the sweetheart of the masquerade warehouse industry, it was not nearly as warmly received by those hosting the entertainments. Restricting the domino from non-commercial masquerade spaces highlights the *beau monde*'s increasing dependency on the convenience of the habit despite their desire to keep masquerades entertaining and character-filled.

The first domino ban occurred at a masquerade in February 1770 under the direction of Teresa Cornelys, owner of Carlisle House and noted 'empress of pleasure'. Cornelys's house was the site of exclusive entertainments for the *beau monde*, including concerts, gaming, and her famed masquerades. Her lavish taste and ever-changing décor kept her at the top of fashionable spaces in London.[124] Her efforts to limit the domino may have been tied to her desire to remain so and keep her masquerades entertaining and spectacular. Although there are no extant tickets for this particular masquerade, newspapers reported that the restriction was clearly 'expressed in the tickets' but despite this, several dominos still appeared. The *General Evening Post* published an apologetic account of those guilty, among whom were the Dukes of Grafton and Bedford and Lords Camden and Beaulieu as well as the French ambassador, explaining that they simply did not have enough time to dress in anything else.[125] A masquerade held at the Guildhall a month later followed Cornelys's suit and emphasised that 'no dominos will be admitted on any account whatsoever'.[126] There are no records as to whether or not this warning was effective, but the restrictions on dominos seemed to disappear for the remainder of the decade, marking the ban as either successful or repelling elite attendance. Continued reports censuring their overtaking masquerade venues and increasing advertisements to let or purchase dominos suggest the ban was unpopular and ineffective, resulting in its singularity until the 1780s.

The managers of the Pantheon attempted to implement a domino ban in 1782, publicising the dress code in advertisements and on tickets. In the days preceding the entertainment, several newspapers warned, 'No Masques will be admitted but such as are dressed in a character; and no domino on any pretence whatever, to appear in the rooms any time of the night'.[127] Guards stationed at

---

[124] Gillian Russell, *Women, Sociability and Theatre in Georgian London* (Cambridge: Cambridge University Press, 2007) 43–8; Judith Summers, *Empress of Pleasure: The Life and Adventures of Teresa Cornelys* (London: Penguin Books, 2004), 200–9.

[125] *General Evening Post*, 1–3 March 1770.   [126] *Independent Chronicle* 12–14 March 1770.

[127] *Morning Herald and Daily Advertiser*, 13 April 1782.

the entrance to the masquerade reinforced this restriction – not only did they help to ensure the masquerade remained orderly, they also worked as effective costume censors. Their responsibility was taken seriously and they did not hesitate to deny dominos entrance, regardless of ticket possession or rank. One particular instance involved Lord Peterborough being refused admission due to his wearing a black domino. Until he removed the domino, he was kept from entering the masquerade.[128] This interaction is almost identical to the earlier incidence involving Carlisle House and Dukes Grafton and Bedford and company. When examined together, the rank and gender of those breaching the rules of dress stand out rather clearly: they are all men of rank. While the ban may have been put in place to encourage everyone to dress in character and give as much as they received in the entertainment, elite men chose to remain wilfully ignorant of this and decided their status would be enough to get them through the doors despite flouting the restriction. In the case of the Pantheon masquerade and Lord Peterborough, this was not so. His being stopped shows that the ban was taken seriously and would have similarly impacted the participation of those using a domino for convenience or affordability. The preference for drawing character dress to the masquerade in these two instances and subsequent banning of domino costume not only would have kept middling professions and 'boring' dominos out of masquerade spaces but also indicated the presence of an audience and significance of the entertainment as one of display and differentiation.[129]

King's Theatre also implemented a restriction on dress, advertising their 'Grand Masked Ball (Parèe), In which Fancy Dresses and Coloured Dominos (Black excepted) will be admitted'.[130] The decision to admit entry to coloured dominos provided a compromise of sorts; it allowed those attracted to domino habits to join the entertainment, and while it did not guarantee an increase in conviviality and character appearances, it would improve the overall masquerade scene with a spectrum of colours other than the drab black. This dress code had been circulating roughly two weeks prior to the date of the masquerade; however, upon the arrival of the masquerade, King's issued an updated notice that included a considerable change. As of that day, black dominos would be acceptable and allowed to participate in the masquerade after all.[131] While the motivation behind this revision is unclear, there are a few possible reasons that may have been singularly or jointly responsible for this change. Given the year of the masquerade, 1797, and the price of the ticket, 10s 6d, King's may have been attempting to maintain a semblance of exclusivity to their 'Grand Masked

---

[128] *Morning Herald and Daily Advertiser*, 23 April 1782.
[129] Kobza, 'The Habit of Habits', 276.   [130] *True Briton*, 16 May 1797.
[131] *Oracle and Public Advertiser*, 30 May 1797.

Ball' by limiting the use of the black domino and subsequent attendance of the middling sorts. The ticket price would have made the masquerade more afford- able, and that, plus the opportunity to let a reasonably priced domino, would have opened the gates to a much wider social group than previous years. The belated shift in costume rules may have also been a result of low ticket sales. Publicising this change and suddenly allowing black dominos on the day of the entertainment would now present new opportunities for interested parties to attend without advance plans and hopefully attract more people (and profits) from the masquerade.

Domino bans were not limited to commercial venues; elites who hosted masquerade viewings in their town houses and members of the nobility who held masquerades in their sprawling estates also instituted 'house rules' to keep out the monochromatic menace. Throughout the second half of the century, leading ladies of the *beau monde* hosted viewing parties that preceded masquer- ade evenings. They issued calling cards, which allowed a select number of entries to their London residences in the fashionable areas of Mayfair, Bedford Square, and St James's.[132] As black dominos continued to blight masquerades with their characterless presence, growing in number during the 1790s and 1800s, these women used their viewing parties as a means to help regulate the domino's overuse. In 1794, the *Morning Chronicle* called attention to this, noting that the joint efforts of the 'Ladies of Fashion' were 'ingenious and apt for this purpose . . . which cannot fail to enrich the spectacle [of the masquerade] by gaity'.[133] On several occasions calling cards dictated that no dominos would be admitted, thus discouraging those within the ton who planned to stop along their way to the masquerade from donning dominos (Figure 16). Although a popular and convenient option for disguise, this action highlights that the domino's overuse frustrated those who spent efforts organising the entertain- ment and were regular participants.

Of the fashionable ladies, Mrs Althea Walker had a particular reputation among high society for her lavish entertainments, which included mask view- ings and masquerades.[134] She regularly placed restrictions on dominos, barring black dominos or plain dominos from entry to her residential festivities in 1798, 1800, and 1801.[135] At her masquerade in 1800, the doors opened at eleven o'clock in the evening and over the course of three hours guests continued to

---

[132] This included the Duchess of Ancaster, Mrs Orby-Hunter, Mrs Chichester, and Mrs Broadhead, to name a few.
[133] *Morning Chronicle*, 1 May 1794.
[134] Paul Cooper, 'Mrs Walker's Masquerades 1800–1804', 22 February 2022, *Regency Dances*, www.regencydances.org/paper055.php, accessed 20 October 2022.
[135] *Times*, 18 May 1798; *Times*, 29 May 1800; *Morning Chronicle*, 4 June 1801.

Figure 16 Invitation from Mrs Chichester for a masked ball, 1810

arrive in a range of character costumes and dominos. The *Times* reported that the 'gradual influx had a wonderful effect in heightening the pleasure of the scene. Scarcely had one new character presented itself, when another and another succeeded, and thus the whole night was one continued series of novelty. The exclusion of black dominos aided much the brilliancy of the coup d' ail.'[136] Mrs Walker's masquerade was already an exclusive entertainment as it was invitation only, aligning her repeated decision to restrict black dominos with the wider effort to keep masquerade scenes lively and entertaining. The ban on black dominos did not seem to impinge the presence of colourful dominos, which was still significant. The Prince of Wales and Mrs Fitzherbert wore complimentary dominos of grey and blue while the Duchesses of Devonshire and Cumberland dressed in blue and pink respectively. Orange and white dominos were also present, contributing to a variance of shades that mixed with character and fancy dress to create a more visually appealing entertainment than those plagued with black dominos.

Invitations to private celebrations at country seats and elite family homes also worked to limit the spread of the black domino and pointed to its increasing negative presence and a sense of growing disapproval among the upper ranks. Viscount William Courtenay, later the 9th Earl of Devon, hosted an extravagant masquerade as part of a three-day fête for his coming of age. As a member of the House of Lords and landowner of prominent estates in England and Ireland, Courtenay had wealth (an income of £67,000 per year) and political status.[137]

---

[136] *Times*, 29 May 1800.

[137] 'Music Room Chandelier', the 100 Objects at Powderham Project, University of Plymouth, Cornerstone Praxis with Plymouth University, Powderham Castle, accessed 12 January 2020, www.100objectsproject.com/explore/005-music-room-chandelier.

Despite being the centre of scandalous gossip in 1784, the 9th Earl was a member of the Prince of Wales's set and maintained recognition among the *beau monde* throughout the 1790s.[138] He was known to attend commercial masquerades in London with the Prince of Wales and often opted to wear character or Vandyke dress. His enthusiasm for masquerades was reflected in his hosting similar entertainments in his town house in Grosvenor Square and his country seat in Exeter – Powderham Castle.[139]

The 9th Earl's masquerade in 1790, a part of his birthday celebrations, has left behind a partial paper trail in the form of tickets, a personal account, newspaper reports, and his portrait, each of which give perspective on the 9th Earl's expectations of the masquerade and how black dominos might have been viewed among the elite at this point in the century. The three-day celebration, estimated to have cost approximately £9,000, had an exclusive guest list, temporary structures, and exquisite decorations and illuminations. Invitations were issued in the form of tickets and sent to his 'particular friends' with the instruction that 'upon their being further circulated, the names of the Presenter and Accepter were written on them. This regulation kept the company as select as possible.'[140] The invitation-tickets strongly resembled those of the commercial masquerades in London, to which the earl was no stranger (Figure 17). The inscription across the top includes a ticket number, 428, and additional text, 'Black Dominos not admitted'.[141] This handwritten line has similarly appeared on other tickets for this same masquerade, indicating his awareness that several friends within his set, like the Prince of Wales who was known to order and sport the black domino, might appear clad in the dull dress if not told otherwise. The earl's desire to exclude the black domino from his masquerade indicated that he did not want a dull scene for his giant birthday extravaganza and expected his guests to participate by dressing in either colourful embellished dominos or character costumes, as he himself frequently wore. Like other elites who attempted to keep the domino from their residences and larger masquerade scenes, the 9th Earl successfully dictated the dress code of this masquerade to fit his own preferences, presenting the entertainment as one that was often shaped by the elite whether in London or on the periphery. Like the viewings and masquerades in London, entry to this entertainment was closely monitored through personally issued invitations and would have been exclusive, making

---

[138] His aristocratic rank may have also made him a more prominent figure among gossip – particularly concerning his widely rumoured same-sex attraction.

[139] *Public Advertiser*, 27 April 1790; *Public Advertiser*, 16 February 1792.

[140] *Public Advertiser*, 7 August 1790.

[141] Two tickets at the British Museum: C,2.1213 and C,2.1046.

Figure 17 Ticket to Lord Courtenay's masquerade and supper at Powderham Castle, 1790 © The Trustees of the British Museum. All rights reserved.

the domino's middling associations unimportant and highlighting the ban was more about entertainment and spectacle than social infiltration.

Other members of the elite, including members of the royal family and peerage, also deployed domino restrictions on masquerades held at their residences and social spaces. Cousin to George III, the royal highnesses the Margrave and Margravine of Anspach, Charles Alexander and his second wife, Elizabeth Craven, were not warmly welcomed into elite society and hosted extravagant parties that brought them into fashionable social networks. Their dinners and parties at Brandenburg House in Hammersmith often included guests from notable families throughout England, including the Delavals, the Dukes of Clarence and St Albans, and Lord and Lady Dormer.[142] Two existing invitations to one of these elaborate entertainments made clear their stance on black dominos, warning guests 'Nobody admitted . . .

---

[142] Details of other entertainments in newspaper clippings in the British Museum (C,2.1043; C,2.1044). Banks collection.

with Black Dominos'.[143] Royalty likewise supported and attended the Union Club, which employed a domino ban at a masquerade they held in 1802. This private organisation was housed in Cumberland House, a former noble residence. Key members of the club included the Dukes of Norfolk and Bedford, Richard Sheridan, and Charles Fox – most of whom had previously attended several masquerades wearing dominos.[144] Despite their and their peers' past dependence on the domino, tickets clearly stated 'No Dominos Admitted' across the bottom as a reminder to participants.[145] This shift away from the domino in a male-dominated space of sociability suggests an increasing disapproval of the domino and reflects the beginning movement toward fancy dress parties, which gradually replaced masquerades toward the end of the Regency period.

4.3 The Domino Nowhere

As the preceding section has shown, reports and accounts of dominos at masquerades surfaced consistently throughout the second half of the century indicating that the domino was a sizeable fixture within masquerade scenes and as such often viewed as a problem by those who hosted the extravagant entertainments. Likewise, the domino appeared in portraiture and satire, where it was employed as a tool and recognisable symbol of the masquerade. Taking these perspectives into consideration, it is very peculiar that the domino is either nearly absent or grossly under-represented in popular depictions of masquerade scenes. Regardless of the artist, year, and masquerade, these images consistently underrepresent the attendance of dominos otherwise present in newspapers and manuscript accounts. This is seen in popular prints of the masquerade that circulated as illustrations alongside masquerade reports in periodicals, singular items, and on commemorative masquerade handkerchiefs. These depictions of the masquerade provide a different reality of the masquerade, suggesting that the domino was absent from the entertainment, and contribute to the creation of an idealised version of the entertainment – one that aligned with anticipatory expectations and cultural tropes rather than reality. The noticeable lack of dominos across representational masquerade references indicates that there were considerable discrepancies between what people thought happened at masquerades and what actually occurred. Contemporary

---

[143] The tickets for Brandenburg House exist in the collections of the British Museum (1897,1231.292) and the Museum of London (80.457/3).

[144] 'Records of the Union Club', London Metropolitan Archives, https://search.lma.gov.uk/scripts/mwimain.dll/144/LMA_OPAC/web_detail/REFD+A~2FUNC?SESSIONSEARCH, accessed 15 September 2022.

[145] The Union Club ticket is in the collections of the British Museum (C,2.1248).

depictions sought to capture the extraordinary, jovial, and unruly aspects of the masquerade, which would in turn attract consumers and impact the reputation of the entertainment within eighteenth-century culture.

Broad sweeping scenes of masquerades in various venues also spread visual impressions of the entertainment. The work of the elite Venetian artist, Canaletto, inspired several prints and drawings of a masquerade scenes at Ranelagh Gardens during the 1750s and 1760s (Figures 10 and 12).[146] The first engraving (Figure 10) commemorates a celebratory birthday masquerade, as written across the top of the image. The foreground is filled with jolly masqueraders who represented those in attendance and exhibit a fanciful ward-robe of habits. Among the various dresses are harlequins, oriental costume, quakers, a shepherdess, clowns, Vandyke dress, highlanders, and an old hag. The immediate placement of these entertaining characters along the foreground suggests the masquerade as an entertaining pastime with dominos absent upon first glance. Closer inspection of the piece reveals the few dominos lurking behind these central characters in the space between the Rotunda and front line of masqueraders. Four dominos are clearly represented wearing the traditional cloak, mask draped with fabric, and tricorn hat (one on the far left and three evenly spaced across the centre line) (Figure 11). Their presence is hardly reflective of the criticisms in the press and comments of Horace Walpole, which suggest many dominos are excluded from the print. The second Ranelagh scene, also after Canaletto, shows a similar set of characters and includes only one easily recognisable domino figure. He is dressed in a blue domino with a red waistcoat and stands on the far left side of the landscape (Figure 13). His singular appearance suggests to the viewer that masquerades were varied and colourful experiences, filled with entertaining characters, and that it was more popular to dress as a character than a domino.

This practice continued into later masquerade scenes of other venues, includ-ing Carlisle House and the Pantheon. One of the earliest illustrations of the masquerades at Carlisle House was printed in 1771 as part of the *Oxford Magazine*. It was smaller in scale than the sweeping scenes after Canaletto, limiting the artist in who and what they could include in the illustration to best convey the spirit of the masquerade. The title of the piece indicates the focus on the 'remarkable characters' at a Cornelys masquerade, and the artist decisively displayed only those that fit the titular criteria (Figure 18). The image circulated the magazine alongside a brief report of the masquerade, bringing to life the most colourful and notable costumes for the reader with a particular focus on the

---

[146] Link to original Canaletto: www.christies.com/en/lot/lot-5106183.

Figure 18 *Remarkable Characters at Mrs. Cornely's Masquerade*, 1771,
courtesy of the Lewis Walpole Library, Yale University

curious costume of the coffin.[147] Newspaper reports of the same masquerade also drew attention to the coffin, as well as the she-bear, but equally noted that apart from these characters, 'there did not appear to be a great degree of taste in the dresses, especially those of the men, who mostly went in dominos'.[148] Unlike the newspaper reports, the illustration and accompanying text completely omit the domino from the masquerade scene. There are no visual hints of the domino in the foreground or background and the letter to the editor makes no mention of the habit either. While the title of the illustration indicates that the main subject is those in remarkable dress, the complete absence of this symbolic and apparently overworn habit points to a discrepancy between the actual experience of the masquerade and the expectation of attending one.

Two prints of masquerades at the Pantheon, issued in 1773 and 1809 respectively, leave the domino out of the foreground and challenge the viewer to find any of sign of the familiar habit in the scene. The earlier engraving of the Pantheon presents the usual cast of characters and those in the foreground are drawn with careful attention to detail (Figure 19). The year of the earlier engraving indicates that many dominos would have been in attendance, as the

---

[147] 'To the Editor of the Oxford Magazine (With a Copper-Plate of Characters at Mrs. Cornelly's Masquerade', *Oxford Magazine*, Vol VI, February 1771, 64.
[148] *General Evening Post*, 5–7 February 1771.

Figure 19 Charles White, *A Masquerade Scene at the Pantheon*, 1773

first attempt to ban the domino happened in 1770 and newspapers were rife with complaints of the habit by this point. There are two dominos lurking in the upper right gallery of the Pantheon, easily identified by their feathered hats, draping masks, and dark, non-descript cloaks, but they hardly represent the larger presence of the 'insipid mask'.[149] The date of creation places this image amidst the fervour of complaints and growing warehouse advertisements for dominos, hinting that it is not meant to be an accurate portrayal of the masquerade but rather an idealised one. Rowlandson's Pantheon engraving likewise depicts the popular stock characters of the masquerade in the foreground and fills the space with lively masqueraders of all varieties dancing and revelling throughout the venue (Figure 20). The masqueraders making up the background and hanging from the galleries, while harder to identify, do not provide any visual clues of wearing dominos leaving the habit missing from the scene.

The commemorative handkerchief was another aspect of eighteenth-century masquerade culture that excluded the domino from its portrayals of masquerade scenes. The practical use and ephemeral nature of these objects has resulted in few remaining examples, with one in the Museum of London and one in the Victoria and Albert Museum. These objects represent two different

---

[149] *The Gazetteer and New Daily Advertiser*, 29 May 1772.

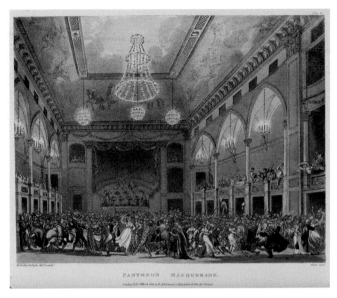

Figure 20 Thomas Rowlandson, *Pantheon Masquerade*, 1809, courtesy of the
Lewis Walpole Library, Yale University

masquerades, one at Ranelagh Gardens and the other at Carlisle House in Soho
Square, suggesting that it was not uncommon to commemorate the entertainment through accessible, portable paraphernalia. Associated with the increasing
practice of taking snuff and invention of pockets, decorative and commemorative handkerchiefs shifted from being worn on the shoulders and around the
neck to fashionable accessories that represented one's taste and social status.[150]
The handkerchief's use as a personal item subsequently carried the masquerade
into quotidian spaces of sociability, leaving the domino and otherwise dull
aspects of the entertainment behind.

    The first handkerchief depicted a masquerade scene within Ranelagh
Gardens near the Chinese Pavilion, in the style of previous masquerade prints
(Figure 21 for handkerchief, Figure 11 for print). The print was not satirical in
nature, but rather a portrayal of the event, or a similar one, at the gardens. It
included imagery of a variety of costumes, ranging from oriental themes to
classical *commedia dell'arte* dress. Along the top of the handkerchief was the
inscription 'A Representation of the KING of DENMARK'S Masquerade in
Ranelagh Gardens', dating the souvenir to 1768. The Danish King, Christian
VII, hosted several masquerades during his tour of England, which were all

---

[150] Linda Eaton, *Printed Textiles: British and American Cottons and Linens 1700–1850*
(New York: Monacelli Press, 2014), 340–7.

Figure 21 King of Denmark's masquerade, handkerchief, 1768, Museum of London

reported as grand entertainments attended by none but 'persons of the best quality'.[151] The handkerchief, like the Ranelagh prints, circulated an idealised depiction of the masquerade, leaving the domino out of the scene. It would have memorialised the exciting moments of the masquerade to those who attended and represented a diverse and entertaining scene one might hope to encounter if they had not. Circulation of this print in handkerchief form also suggests that it was an acceptable depiction that could appeal to the wider public.

The second handkerchief shares some design components with the first; it was printed in blue, included the location of the masquerade, and illustrated a series of characters that might be in attendance (Figure 22). The differences, however, are perhaps more illuminating in considering the misrepresentation of the domino despite its widespread recognition as a symbol of the masquerade. Unlike the handkerchief from the Museum of London, this one does not commemorate a royal event nor does it portray a wide masquerade scene. Instead, it depicts sixteen individual masquerade characters that are associated

---

[151] King Christian hosted at least two masquerades in 1768 – one at Ranelagh in July and one at King's Theatre in October. He is also reported to have attended a masquerade at Carlisle House in his final week in London.

Figure 22 Print of Soho Square grand masquerade, handkerchief, c.1771,
© Victoria and Albert Museum, London

with the 'Present Taste of the Nobility and Gentry', as indicated in the text running along the border. While these characters appear in newspaper reports and personal accounts of masquerades with some receiving more attention than others, like Harlequin, the Old Witch, and the Highlander, none come close to the circulation of the domino habit. Tying these characters and the masquerade to the upper ranks again presents a disjunction between the recorded experience of the entertainment and representations of it in visual and material culture. As newspapers, periodicals, correspondence, and diaries show, the domino was a highly popular choice among the elite from the 1760s through the end of the century. Omitting the domino from this display indicates there was an active choice to edit how the masquerades at Cornelys's house were depicted. This may have been driven by a combination of factors, including Cornelys's desire to circulate a specific image of her entertainments. Presenting various characters in association with her masquerades would imply they were entertaining and encourage people to attend. The range of characters also exhibits possible costume options that could serve as inspiration for those who would have otherwise chosen a domino. These features make the handkerchief more engaging and appealing to the consumer and highlight the intended performative component of the masquerade. The handkerchief also includes a brief phrase across the top, which provides additional insight into the intentions of the entertainment and absence of the domino. '*Spectatus admissi risum teneatis amici*', when translated, becomes 'Can even the friends who are admitted to see the work [spectacle] refrain from laughter', suggesting the masquerade was a selective space for enjoyment, playfulness, and sociability – none of which were components of the domino habit. Excluding the domino from this and other depictions of the masquerade arguably functioned in a similar way to the domino bans; both recognised that the domino habit created dull scenes and its presence should be discouraged. These depictions show what a domino-free masquerade could be while also circulating imagined rather than actual representations of the masquerade.

While it is important to analyse the prints and handkerchiefs as individual objects, their broader commonalities signify a new cultural understanding of the masquerade that has received little attention in previous scholarship. These pieces do not adhere to the cultural trope of the masquerade as a debaucherous and socially transgressive space nor do they present it as a satire. They are artistic depictions of contemporary costumes and experiences at the entertainment. Their movement through the consumer market indicated a demand for masquerade-related objects that presented a curated representation of the entertainment and that could be used to display fashionable taste and socio-economic status, whether or not the consumer attended the masquerade in reality. The under-representation of the domino across these various sources shows that the domino was not accidentally overlooked, but rather actively excluded or minimised in popular portrayals. Sweeping scenes made it clear that the subject was a masquerade – this was indicated verbally through the specific label of 'masquerade' in the titles and the collective presence of stock characters and intermittent masks. The domino, in these instances, might have been an understood component of the masquerade and, mirroring the sentiments of the newspaper critics, artists felt that its appearance would detract from rather than enhance the visual spectacle and tone of the entertainment.

Conclusion

At once both convenient and contentious, the domino was a central part of eighteenth-century masquerade culture in London. Examining the domino through the lenses of material, visual, and print culture has revealed the popular masquerade habit to have been a multifaceted garment that was a costume, commodity, or nuisance. Its variability made it an attractive disguise, offering the upper ranks an easy opportunity to flaunt their status and wealth through embellishment while giving the middling sorts a relatively affordable costume required to attend this once-in-a-lifetime entertainment. The materiality and physicality of the three surviving dominos has highlighted how the customisa bility of the habit suited the needs of the wearer, allowing them to display taste through dress. The domino's ability to be quickly altered and its equally appealing ease of wear were ideal for the nobility and gentry who attended masquerades regularly throughout the fashionable season and grew tired of always dressing in character.

Their increasing use of this habit coincided with the peak of masquerade culture when ticket and costume prices were at their highest. It was at this point that the domino became a profitable staple in masquerade warehouses, where it grew into a key symbol of the masquerade itself. Warehouse owners gave dominos consistent attention in their advertisements and used language and price to encourage new and continued custom. Tracing the shifts in domino language and price reflected the delayed commercialisation of the masquerade despite the trends of widening accessibility that other forms of leisure culture were experiencing at the time. These descriptions and the itemised inventory list of James Spilsbury contributed to a landscape of masquerade culture and complement the evidence from the three existing dominos, which share several of the main material characteristics (colour, fabric, embellishments, richness). Combined, these sources emphasise the value of the domino as a commodity within the warehouse industry and show how it operated primarily within the price range of the nobility and gentry, contributing to the masquerade's pro-longed existence as a space for elite sociability.

Warehouse advertisements implied a regular demand for the domino that was substantiated through their recurring presence in personal accounts of masquer-ades and newspaper reports that circulated in the days following an entertain-ment. The relative indifference to the domino evidenced in correspondence and diaries sits in opposition to the overwhelming criticism the domino continually received in the press. This disjunction is further evidence of the domino holding different cultural and social meanings that were shaped by status, spatial context, and personal opinion. While the domino was an attractive costume option for the elite and middling sorts, it was a nuisance to masquerade hosts and artists who hoped to provide a colourful and lively experience for their patrons. Attempts to ban the domino from physical spaces and minimise its presence in visual representations indicate that, as many newspapers stated, the domino was dull and negatively impacted the masquerade. The desire to remove the domino, either completely or in part, implies its overwhelming presence and therefore alters the existing narrative on the cultural significance of the mas-querade. While costume might have allowed some the opportunity to transgress social boundaries and gender norms, the cost of a domino, its consistent popularity, and the action against it indicate that the masquerade was predominately an exclusionary space that reinforced the existing social hierarchy despite wider trends in the commercialisation of leisure.

Ultimately, the domino was everywhere and nowhere. It was a cloak of convenience for the elite and an affordable disguise for the middling sorts. It was a profitable commodity for warehouses and a problematic plague for masquerade hosts. It was plain and ostentatious, rich and shabby, black and colourful. Examining the domino as it moved from body to venue to paper has established it as a central component of both the real and imagined masquerade experience. Uncovering the complexity of the domino and its relationship to the masquerade through an interdisciplinary approach proves that even the dullest object can reveal a dazzling new perspective.

Bibliography

Primary Sources

Manuscript Sources

Alnwick Castle, Private Papers of the Duke of Northumberland
    121/5a, Diaries of Elizabeth Percy, Duchess of Northumberland
    121/31a, Diaries of Elizabeth Percy, Duchess of Northumberland
    121/174, Cloaths Account, Duchess of Northumberland
Bedfordshire Archives
    L30/14/435/12, Wrest Park Papers
Essex Record Office
    D/DWt/A1, Household Bills and Vouchers of Thomas Whitmore
Royal Archives at Windsor Castle
    GEO/MAIN/29315
Wiltshire and Swindon Archives
    9/35/316, Twenty-five letters from James Brudenell to his brother Thomas, 4th Earl of Ailesbury

Printed Primary Sources

Anonymous. *Dictionarium Britannicum*. 2nd ed. London: T. Cox, 1730.
    Johnson's Dictionary of the English Language in Miniature. 8th ed. London: Lee and Hurst, 1797.
    A new English dictionary. London: Robert Knaplock at Bishop's Head, 1713.
Burney, Frances. *Cecilia, Or, Memoirs of an Heiress. by the Author of Evelina. in Five Volumes*, edited by Peter Sabor and Margaret Anne Doody. Oxford: Oxford University Press, 2008.
    The Early Diary of Frances Burney, Vol.1, 1768–1773, edited by Lars E. Troide. Oxford: Clarendon, 1988. London: G. Bell and Sons, 1889.
A Catalogue of the genuine, rich and very extensive Wardrobe Consisting of a Great Variety of Masquerade Dresses, the Property of Mr. Spilsbury . . . London: Christie's Auction House, 1779.
Climenson, Emily J., ed. *Passages from the Diaries of Mrs. Phillip Lybbe Powys*. London: Longmans, Green, and Co., 1899.
Fielding, Henry. *Amelia*. In *The Wesleyan Edition of the Works of Henry Fielding*, edited by Martin C. Battestin. Oxford: Oxford University Press, 1984.

George, Prince of Wales. 'Letter to Frederick'. In *The Correspondence of George Prince of Wales 1770–1821*, edited by Arthur Aspinall. London: Cassell, 1963.

Walpole, Horace. *The Yale Edition of Horace Walpole's Correspondence*. New Haven: Yale University Press, 1937–83.

London Newspapers and Periodicals

Argus
Gazetteer and New Daily Advertiser
General Advertiser and Morning Intelligencer
General Evening Post
Independent Chronicle
London Chronicle
London Courant and Westminster Chronicle
London Evening Post
Middlesex Journal or Chronicle of Liberty
Morning Chronicle
Morning Chronicle and London Advertiser
Morning Herald
Morning Herald and Daily Advertiser
Morning Post
Morning Post and Daily Advertiser
Morning Post and Fashionable World
Oracle and Public Advertiser
Oxford Magazine
Public Advertiser or Political and Literary Diary
St James' Chronicle or the British Evening Post
Times
True Briton
World

Secondary Sources

Published Secondary Sources

Alexander, Kimberly S. *Treasures Afoot: Shoe Stories from the Georgian Era*. Baltimore: Johns Hopkins University Press, 2018.

Anishanslin, Zara. *Portrait of a Woman in Silk: Hidden Histories of the British Atlantic World*. New Haven: Yale University Press, 2016.

Berg, Maxine. *Luxury and Pleasure in Eighteenth-Century Britain*. Oxford: Oxford University Press, 2005.

Bermingham, Ann and John Brewer, eds. *The Consumption of Culture 1600–1800: Image, Object, Text*. London: Routledge, 1995.

Berry, Helen. 'Polite Consumption: Shopping in Eighteenth-Century England'. *Transactions of the Royal Historical Society* 12 (2002): 375–94.

Black, Jeremy. *The English Press in the Eighteenth Century*. Beckenham: Croom Helm, 1987.

Borsay, Peter. 'The Emergence of a Leisure Town: Or an Urban Renaissance?' *Past & Present* 126 (February 1990): 189–96.

Brewer, John. *The Pleasures of the Imagination: English Culture in the Eighteenth Century*. London: HarperCollins, 1997.

Brewer, John and Roy Porter, eds. *Consumption and the World of Goods*. London: Routledge, 1993.

Burke, Peter. *Popular Culture in Early Modern Europe*. London: Harper and Row, 1978.

Castle, Terry. *Masquerade and Civilization: The Carnivalesque in Eighteenth-Century English Culture and Fiction*. Stanford: Stanford University Press, 1986.

Craft-Fairchild, Catherine. *Masquerade and Gender: Disguise and Female Identity in Eighteenth-Century Fictions by Women*. Pennsylvania: Pennsylvania State University Press, 1993.

Doderer-Winkler, Melanie. *Magnificent Entertainments: Temporary Architecture for Georgian Festivals*. London: Yale University Press, 2013.

Dyer, Serena. 'State of the Field: Material Culture'. *History* 106, no. 370 (2021): 282–92.

Dyer, Serena and Chloe Wigston Smith, eds. *Material Literacy in Eighteenth-Century Britain: A Nation of Makers*. London: Bloomsbury, 2020.

Earle, Peter. 'The Middling Sort in London'. In *The Middling Sort of People: Culture, Society, and Politics in England, 1550–1800*, edited by Christopher Brooks and Jonathan Barry. London: Macmillan, 1994, 141–58.

Eaton, Linda. *Printed Textiles: British and American Cottons and Linens 1700–1850*. New York: Monacelli Press, 2014.

Eglin, John. *Venice Transfigured: The Myth of Venice in British Culture, 1660–1797*. New York: Palgrave, 2001.

Erickson, Amy Louise. 'Eleanor Mosley and Other Milliners in the City of London Companies 1700–1750'. *History Workshop Journal* 71 (Spring 2011): 147–72.

Gerritsen, Anne and Giorgio Riello. *Writing Material Culture*. London: Bloomsbury Academic, 2015.

Greig, Hannah. "'All Together and All Distinct': Public Sociability and Social Exclusivity in London's Pleasure Gardens, Ca. 1740–1800'. *Journal of British Studies* 51 (2012): 50–75.

Greig, Hannah and Amanda Vickery, eds. 'The Political Day in London, c. 1697–1834'. *Past & Present* 252, no. 1 (2020): 101–37.

Harvey, Karen, ed. *History and Material Culture: A Student's Guide to Approaching Alternative Sources*. New York: Routledge, 2009.

'Men of Parts: Masculine Embodiment and the Male Leg in Eighteenth-Century England'. *Journal of British Studies* 54, October (2015): 797–821.

Hume, Robert D. 'The Value of Money in Eighteenth-Century England: Incomes, Prices, Buying Power – and Some Problems in Cultural Economics'. *Huntington Library Quarterly* 77, no. 4 (2015): 373–416.

Hunt, Margaret. *The Middling Sort: Commerce, Gender, and the Family in England 1680–1780*. Berkeley: University of California Press, 1996.

Hunter, David. 'Rode the 12,000? Counting Coaches, People and Errors En Route to the Rehearsal of Handel's *Music for the Royal Fireworks* at Spring Gardens, Vauxhall in 1749'. *The London Journal* 37, no. 1 (March 2012): 13–26.

Kobza, Meghan. 'Dazzling or Fantastically Dull? Re-examining the Eighteenth-Century London Masquerade'. *Journal for Eighteenth-Century Studies* 43, no. 2 (2020): 161–81.

'The Habit of Habits: Material Culture and the Eighteenth-Century London Masquerade'. *Studies in Eighteenth-Century Culture* 50, no. 1 (2021): 265–93.

Marschner, Joanna and Nigel Arch. *Splendour at Court: Dressing for Royal Occasions since 1700*. London: Unwin Hyman, 1987.

McKendrick, Neil. 'Introduction'. In *The Birth of a Consumer Society: The Commercialization of Eighteenth-Century England*, edited by John Brewer, Neil McKendrick, and J. H. Plumb. London: Europa, 1982.

'George Packwood and the Commercialization of Shaving: The Art of Eighteenth-Century Advertising or "the Way to Get Money and Be Happy"'. In *The Birth of a Consumer Society: The Commercialization of Eighteenth-Century England*, edited by John Brewer, Neil McKendrick, and J. H. Plumb. London: Europa, 1982, 147–9.

McKendrick, Neil, John Brewer, and J.H. Plumb. *The Birth of a Consumer Society: The Commercialization of Eighteenth-Century England*. London: Europa, 1982.

Ribeiro, Aileen. *Dress in Eighteenth-Century Europe: 1715–1789*. London: Yale University Press, 2002.

The Dress Worn at Masquerades in England, 1730 to 1790, and Its Relation to Fancy Dress in Portraiture. London: Garland Publishing, 1984.

Riello, Giorgio. 'Things that Shape History: Material Culture and Historical Narratives'. Chap. 1 in *History and Material Culture: A Student's Guide to Approaching Alternative Sources*, edited by Karen Harvey. London: Routledge, 2009, 24–47.

Rothstein, Natalie. *Silk Designs of the Eighteenth Century in the Collection of the Victoria and Albert Museum, London with a Complete Catalogue*. London: Bulfinch Press, 1990.

Russell, Gillian. *Women, Sociability and Theatre in Georgian London*. Cambridge: Cambridge University Press, 2007.

Schoeser, Mary. *Printed Handkerchiefs*. London: Museum of London, 1988.

Shammas, Carole. 'Changes in English and Anglo-American Consumption from 1550 to 1800'. In *Consumption and the World of Goods*, edited by John Brewer and Roy Porter. London: Routledge, 1993, 177–205.

Stone, Lawrence. 'The Residential Development of the West End of London in the Seventeenth Century'. In *After the Reformation: Essays in Honor of J. H. Hexter*, edited by Barbara Malament. Philadelphia: University of Pennsylvania Press, 1980, 167–212.

Summers, Judith. *Empress of Pleasure: The Life and Adventures of Teresa Cornelys*. London: Penguin Books, 2004.

Van Horn, Jennifer. *The Power of Objects in Eighteenth-Century British America*. Chapel Hill: University of North Carolina Press, 2017.

Vickery, Amanda. *Behind Closed Doors: At Home in Georgian England*. London: Yale University Press, 2009.

'Mutton Dressed as Lamb? Fashioning Age in Georgian England'. *Journal of British Studies* 52, no. 4 (2013): 858–86.

Vickery, Amanda and John Styles, eds. *Gender, Taste, and Material Culture in Britain and North America 1700–1830*. New Haven: Yale University Press, 2006.

Wahrman, Dror. *The Making of the Modern Self: Identity and Culture in Eighteenth-Century England*. London: Yale University Press, 2006.

Wall, Cynthia Sundberg. *The Prose of Things: Transformations of Description in the Eighteenth Century*. London: University of Chicago Press, 2006.

Weatherill, Lorna. *Consumer Behaviour and Material Culture in Britain, 1660–1760*. 2nd ed. London: Routledge, 1996.

Online Sources

Arnold, Janet. 'A Pink Domino c.1760–70 at the Victoria and Albert Museum', Victoria and Albert Museum, 2009, accessed February 2018, https://collec tions.vam.ac.uk/item/O363441/domino-unknown/.

Cooper, Paul. 'Mrs Walker's Masquerades 1800–1804'. Regency Dances. 22 February 2022, accessed 15 October 2022, www.regencydances.org/ paper055.php.

'Domino: 18th Century'. The Met Museum, New York, accessed 7 March 2021, www.metmuseum.org/art/collection/search/90514.

Hoskin, Dawn. 'Considerations on a Handkerchief'. Victoria and Albert Museum Blog. 16 December 2013, accessed 22 January 2020, www .vam.ac.uk/blog/creating-new-europe-1600-1800-galleries/consider ations-handkerchief.

'Music Room Chandelier'. The 100 Objects at Powderham Project, University of Plymouth, Cornerstone Praxis with Plymouth University, Powderham Castle, accessed 12 January 2020, www.100objectsproject.com/explore/ 005-music-room-chandelier.

'Records of the Union Club'. London Metropolitan Archives, accessed 15 September 2022, https://search.lma.gov.uk/scripts/mwimain.dll/144/ LMA_OPAC/web_detail/REFD+A~2FUNC?SESSIONSEARCH.

Tanner, Simon, Trevor Muñoz, and Pich Hemy Ros. 'Measuring Mass Text Digitization Quality and Usefulness: Lessons Learned from Assessing the OCR Accuracy of the British Library's 19th Century Online Newspaper Archive'. *D-Lib Magazine*, July/August 2009. www.dlib.org/dlib/july09/ munoz/07munoz.html, accessed December 2016.

'Trial of Thomas Lawrence ((t17960406-80), April 1769'. *Old Bailey Proceedings Online*, www.oldbaileyonline.org, version 8.0, accessed 15 September 2022.

Email

Morimoto, Marci. 'White Domino'. Email. 2021.

Acknowledgements

I am grateful to all the generous scholars, archivists, and curators who have helped this project come to fruition and the ability to complete this Element during the first year of my Leverhulme Early Career Fellowship. My time spent in the Victoria and Albert Museum with the pink domino was hugely enhanced by the insight of Rebecca Morrison and my working knowledge of the white domino from the Met would be incomplete without the expertise of Marci Morimoto. Likewise, the archivists at the Royal Archives and local record offices have been indispensable in providing scans and copies before and during the pandemic. The ability to incorporate a wide range of figures throughout the publication would not have been possible without funding from the British Society of Eighteenth-Century Studies (Career Development Award) and internal funding from Newcastle University. I am also deeply appreciative of the editorial team; Markman Ellis and Eve Tavor Bannet have shown incredible patience and offered equal encouragement as this Element shifted from abstract to reality. Rebecca Bullard's initial faith in this topic and our ensuing conversations were particularly helpful in the early stages of this project. A final wave of thanks to Stephanie Howard-Smith and Helen Berry, who, after many conversations about this piece, probably know more about the domino than I do. Your thoughts and support helped keep this moving to the finish line.

N.B. To my patient husband, Tom, thank you for allowing me the time and space to write this amidst a transatlantic move and the addition of our small Research Assistant. I couldn't have done it without you.

Cambridge Elements ≡

Eighteenth-Century Connections

A full series listing is available at: www.cambridge.org/EECC

Printed in the United States
by Baker & Taylor Publisher Services